THE FIRST THIRTY

as told to Jillip Naysinthe Paxson
by Greg Forbes Siegman

IDEALIST

ENTERPRISES INC.

*"If life was nothing but straight lines,
it wouldn't be worth living."*
- Greg's Grandma

———

To Mom and Dad

To the overlooked and the underestimated

And to the parents, grandparents,
teachers and substitute teachers
who encourage their kids to dream

More reviews....

There is a workbook based on this story.
It is filled with hundreds of questions
and projects for you, the reader, to consider.
For more information, go to

www.APlaceToSit.com

There is an expanded version of this story.
For more information, go to

www.TheSilhouetteMan.com

THE FIRST THIRTY

as told to Jillip Naysinthe Paxson
by Greg Forbes Siegman

ISBN: 0-9758794-0-5
Library of Congress Control Number: 2004109674

About the Cover:
Photo by Pam Siegman
Concept & design by IdeaList Enterprises Inc.

This book has been printed and bound in the United States of America.
DBTFISF11-10-02NRRIP
Copyright 2005. Greg Forbes Siegman. All Rights Reserved.
Published by IdeaList Enterprises Incorporated

ideaList enterprises inc.
PO Box 101187 - Chicago, IL 60610
www.IdeaListEnterprises.com

The Tempo Cafe
November 10, 2002 - 11:48 p.m.

For the record, the meeting was supposed to begin at eleven-thirty, and for what it's worth, I arrived twenty minutes early to be safe, so by the time it was 11:48 p.m., I'd already been waiting thirty-eight minutes for Greg to walk through that door so I could interview him for the book I was writing about the first thirty years of his life.

Frankly, a conference room around noon would have been a little more my style, but I was just glad we were finally having the meeting.

A month ago, after I'd been chosen to write the book, I *tried* to set up an interview, but it was easier said than done. Instead of meeting with me, Greg sent me a list of names and said to let him know when I spoke with all of them.

I figured they were people who could help give some background for the story -- so I started at the top and began to work my way down -- but I realized pretty quickly that there was a slight problem with the list.

Of the first fifty people I called, a dozen said they had no idea what I was talking about and hung up. The other thirty-eight *weren't even real.*

It seemed like a waste of time, but I kept looking up the names -- all 142 of them. Rumor had it Greg already turned down five other authors who wanted to tell his story. I wasn't about to give him a reason to add me to the list.

Speaking of those other authors, the ones who got turned down, I'm sure a few of them are *still* wondering why Greg chose the person with the *least* impressive resume to write his story.

It's a fair question with an ironic answer -- life isn't always fair.

The fact of the matter is that only one person on the list of people hoping to tell Greg's story used to play catch with him in his backyard twenty-five years ago.

And that would be me.

Given that I've known Greg since I was little, you might wonder why I need to interview him in the first place. After thirty years, I should pretty much know his story, right?

Well, the fact is my old bond with Greg is just that -- an *old* bond.

We had not seen each other since we were little, so the connection might have been enough to help get me chosen to write the story -- but it certainly isn't enough to make me an expert on it.

Let's face it. I knew Greg when he wet himself on a regular basis. What are the chances the boy I knew and the man he has become are even remotely the same? I doubted I'd even recognize the guy.

But to my surprise, when he did finally show up at five minutes before midnight, I spotted him right away. It was actually quite easy. I mean, who else but Greg would show up at a restaurant with a lunchbox in one hand and a gold-painted milkshake glass in the other?

Not that I gave either much thought.

Once I got a good look at the man himself, I forgot all about what he was holding. The same boy who used to run around the backyard until the sun went down now walked *delicately* -- like a banged-up athlete trying to avoid any sudden movement after the game. His skin was pale and lifeless, and he needed a shave. The bags under his eyes looked out of place on the face of a thirty year old -- except that they matched the bags above them. Even the eyes themselves, once described in a magazine as *penetrating*, looked worn and tired -- as if they'd spent far too many nights fighting to stay open. His shirt and pants were wrinkled and at least two sizes too big (in a he-must-have-lost-fifteen-pounds-since-he-bought-them kind of way). His thick mop of brown hair was even gone -- replaced by, well, *nothing*.

During a brief talk by phone a few days ago, he said, "If you don't recognize me when I walk in, just look for the big ears."

At the time, I figured he was joking, but as he sat down at the table, I realized he was not. His ears really did seem to be the only thing that had *not* changed since he was little.

I started to ask the first question on my mind -- *What happened to you?* -- but before I could get out the words, he offered seven of his own.

"Mind if I take off my shoes?"

I was going to object, for the sake of the other customers, but before I could respond, he had already leaned over to remove them, revealing two mismatched socks in the process.

I stared at (and smelled) his feet in silence until he spoke again.

"Sorry I'm late," he said, "I went to a film and lost all track of time."

I didn't appreciate that he was late -- especially not when his excuse turned out to be something as unimportant as seeing a movie -- but I wanted to get my mind off his feet, was equally anxious to get started with the interview and this seemed like as good a topic as any to break the ice, so I asked, "What did you see?"

He laughed and said, "You really want *that* to be your one question?"

"Excuse me?" I asked.

"Did I forget to mention that?" Greg asked, as he fiddled with his ears. "You're only allowed to ask me one question."

"Says who?" I protested.

"Says me," he replied matter-of-factly.

At first, I figured he was kidding. He couldn't possibly expect me to get all the information I needed to write an entire book by asking just one question. And yet, judging by the look on Greg's face, it was clear that he was serious. After making me show up at a twenty-four hour cafe in the middle of the night (not to mention, making me spend three weeks calling people who didn't exist), he was only going to let me ask *one question*.

"I can't do it," I said with a shrug. "I give up."

"Oh, come on," he pleaded. "You can't give up *that* easy."

Despite my frustration, I couldn't help chuckling. It was just like when we were little. He liked to win as much as the next kid, but more than anything, he just liked to play the game.

"Fine," I said with a smile, "but I'm going to have to think about this for a second. It's not too easy reducing thirty years to just one question."

While the waitress came over and took his order -- a vanilla milkshake and a grilled cheese sandwich -- I sat quietly and thought about his riddle. What one question could get you all the information you need to write a book about the first thirty years of someone's life?

I couldn't think of a good one off the top of my head, but I knew that with most problems in life, as long as you don't get too frustrated and quit, the solution will eventually come to you. And, sure enough, that's what happened in this case. By the time Greg had his meal, I had my question.

"Greg," I said, while he carefully dipped the tip of his straw into the shake to measure its thickness like a little boy using his big toe to check the temperature of the water in a pool, "I've come up with my question."

"Oh yeah?" he replied, as he nibbled on his sandwich. "Let's hear it."

"Will you start at the beginning?"

Judging by the smile on his face, I had apparently solved the riddle.

And so, as the clock struck midnight and the first thirty years of his life came to an end, Greg sat up straight, wiped a couple crumbs off his face, cleared his throat and did as I asked -- he started at the beginning.

THE BEGINNING

On November 10, 1972, a 30 year old stockbroker named Mark and his wife, Rose, had their first child. The boy's first name, Gregory, was chosen in memory of a late relative (whose first name started with a G). The middle name, Forbes, was thought up by Mark in honor of billionaire Malcolm Forbes. Mark had never actually met the famous businessman, but he hoped the name would inspire his son to that same level of success.

The young couple was excited to have their first child. Rose spent hour after hour, day after day, watching and caring for their new baby boy -- and Mark did the same after returning home from work each night.

A year later, Mark and Rose had a baby girl named Michelle. They intended to divide their time evenly between their two kids, but that plan quickly changed -- and with good reason. Michelle was gravely ill.

For the better part of a year, Rose practically lived by her baby's side at the hospital -- with Mark joining them each night after spending the day at the office.

In the meantime, with his parents so focused on his new sister's health, Greg was usually dropped off at his Grandma's. Given his age, the two didn't have any real conversations -- but as she rocked him back and forth on her lap, an unspoken bond did seem to develop between them.

Thanks to some amazing doctors, Greg's little sister eventually pulled through, things got back to 'normal' and the family of four moved into a two story home on a quiet, little street in the suburbs.

The three bedrooms were upstairs -- one for Greg, one for Michelle and one for their parents. Greg's window overlooked the backyard -- a square of grass and bushes enclosed by a white fence. In the far corner, across from Greg's window, there was some jungle gym equipment.

One piece was a giant horse standing on its hind legs. Its back was a ladder that could be climbed up and down. The other piece was a fifteen foot tall, multi-colored stick figure man with his arms stretched out to the side, a swing hanging down from each one. Greg was especially fascinated at night when the man's many colors were draped by the darkness -- turning him into a towering silhouette rising up into the sky.

Sometimes, Greg swung on the swings or climbed the ladder, but on most afternoons, he seemed content to just sit cross-legged and barefoot (he almost never wore shoes) and watch them -- waiting for the moment when the man and the horse finally *moved*. The rest of the time, he played with his dad's dogs or sat up in his room, trying to learn how to read.

Greg's belief that The Ladder Horse and The Silhouette Man might move like real people was just the tip of the iceberg when it came to his imagination. In fact, the boy spent so much time day-dreaming -- and got so distracted by ideas floating through his head -- that he kept running into things. At one point, his dad even gave him a helmet to wear around the house, so he'd stop hurting his head when he bumped into the walls.

When Mark came home from work each night, the family sat down in the kitchen for dinner -- but it was never much of a unified event. Greg's parents and his sister ate one thing, he always ate another.

No matter how hard anyone tried to convince him otherwise, Greg stubbornly insisted on eating just seven things: hot dogs without mustard, peanut butter without jelly, bagels without lox, french toast without syrup, cereal with no milk (so he could eat it with his hands) and grilled cheese sandwiches (which he insisted on calling *meatless cheeseburgers*).

And that was it. *Every* meal of *every* day, it had to be one of those seven things. (Greg's mom did have one small victory. Hoping to fatten up her frail son, she convinced him vanilla milkshakes were filled with special paint that kept teeth bright and shiny.)

Once Greg started school, it did not take long for the older kids to make fun of his eating habits, but it was hardly the only thing they mocked. Right off the bat, he was teased about the way he looked.

He had buck teeth and the kind of chubby cheeks that led people to believe he was always hiding acorns in his mouth. He also had *enormous* ears -- the kind normally seen in cartoons. He tried to comb his hair over them or hide them under hats, but nothing ever worked. Sooner or later, they always managed to pop back out.

And then there was that middle name. Forbes wasn't like John or David. It was *different*. Greg's parents tried to explain it was different *in a good way*. His Grandma even went so far as to tell him he had the *world's greatest name* -- but it was no use. To Greg, it was just one more thing on a never-ending list of things that people teased him about. He eventually started to pretend he had no middle name at all.

To top it off, whenever he got nervous, he peed on himself.

He really was an easy target for teasing if there ever was one.

Despite Greg's problems, there *was* one thing that did go his way. His teachers. Year after year, he had some of the nicest ones a kid could hope for. They were kind and patient and never teased him about anything (or let anyone else tease him in front of them, either). Other than his bedroom and the backyard, the classroom quickly became his favorite place to be.

But that's not to say the teasing stopped completely.

Before and after school, when the teachers weren't there to protect him, Greg still had to fend for himself against the older kids.

As the weeks passed, he began to appreciate the peace and quiet of his backyard more than ever. It became his own private hiding spot -- the one place where he could go outside without ever having to worry about running into the older kids. Before long, the jungle gym equipment out back -- The Silhouette Man and The Ladder Horse -- became his *friends*, and Greg talked to them for hours at a time.

(In later years, people teased Greg for talking too much -- unaware it could be traced directly to the fact that, as a child, he spent hours carrying on conversations with two 'friends' who never said a word.)

When Mark found out his son talked to the jungle gym equipment, he was none too pleased. Hoping to see Greg put his time to better use, he gave him a smock and a brush and said, "Instead of talking to the ladder and the swing set, why don't you paint some pictures of them?"

Greg did as his father told him, but the results were not too impressive. No matter how hard he tried, he could barely draw a straight line. He was on the verge of giving up when his Grandma stepped in.

"You're right, you *stink* at drawing," she said in her no-nonsense way, "but so what? You learn more from your mistakes than you learn when you get it right. So all that really matters is you don't give up. If life was nothing but straight lines, it wouldn't be worth living."

He followed her advice -- and not only with drawing. When he first tried to read, the words got all scrambled up in his head, but instead of giving up, he just kept trying. And sure enough, over time, the words started falling in place and the pages started turning a little faster.

It was an experience that shaped the first lesson of Greg's young life.

*(1) Work twice as long as the people you think
are twice as smart and eventually, you'll catch up*

Once Greg learned to read, he never wanted to stop. He read in the morning before anyone else woke up, and he read after his mom tucked him in at night -- hiding beneath his covers with a little flashlight.

On the weekends, he stayed at the public library for as long as they were open -- going through one book after another after another.

The people he was reading about and the things they did and the places they went filled his imagination with ideas and carried him far away from the "real" world where he never felt quite like he belonged.

Of the books he read, one of his favorites was a book about the Dallas Cowboys. Greg wanted to be just like them. He started running around the yard, wearing that football helmet his parents gave him, playing imaginary games against imaginary friends -- until his dad decided he was old enough to play *real* games with *real* people and signed him up for tee ball (which is when he first became friends with a kid named Charlie).

Shel Silverstein's books of poetry captured Greg's attention, too. With a different poem every few pages, they were a perfect fit for a boy who got so easily distracted.

The Little Engine That Could was another top pick. The story shared the same message his Grandma always delivered -- don't quit.

Another one of Greg's favorites was *Where the Wild Things Are* -- a book about a boy who is magically transported to another land with giant creatures. After reading the story, Greg became *convinced* The Silhouette Man and The Ladder Horse in his backyard could come to life -- no matter what anyone said about them being just metal and paint. And so, at night, he sat in bed, staring out the window, hoping and watching and waiting for the moment they started to move like other real people do.

Greg's *favorite* book was about Harriet Tubman -- partly because it was the first book he ever bought himself (at a grade school book fair), and partly because he was so inspired by her story.

Harriet was a woman who escaped slavery, then spent her life helping others escape, too. The son of a white, suburban businessman obviously could never *really* understand what it was like for a black woman to live through slavery a hundred years earlier, but in his own little-kid-kind-of-way, Greg aspired to be just like Harriet. He wanted to help people, too.

So when, just a few weeks later, a visitor came to his school and talked about a program where kids could help fight a disease by getting people to donate money for every book they read, he quickly signed up.

Rose was not quite as excited. She thought it was a nice charity, and she thought the chance to read books to help it was tailor-made for Greg -- but going out and asking people to donate money for every book he read? Her son was simply too shy to do it. Or so she thought.

Determined to make a difference, he set aside his insecurity, laced up his shoes and headed outside -- walking all over town, knocking on doors, asking anyone and everyone to make a pledge.

Friends, neighbors, strangers, old, young, it didn't matter who they were -- if they crossed his path, he asked for their support. And despite his age and inexperience, he proved to be unusually good at doing it.

Some people were persuaded to give a one-time donation of twenty or thirty dollars. Most of the time, though, they pledged a certain amount for every book he read -- usually fifty cents or a dollar per book -- which motivated him to read even more than ever. While other kids finished a book a week, Greg knocked out one *a day*. He was suddenly raising hundreds of dollars...*at the age of six*.

It was the first time he'd ever felt like he did something well -- and once the ball was rolling, there was just no stopping him. He was a shake-slurping, book-reading, money-raising machine. By the time he was eight, the total was in the thousands instead of the hundreds.

Champ Reader declared the headline in the paper after the charity honored Greg at a special luncheon.

The attention was nice, but the far more lasting reward was what he learned from the process of sitting in his room and at the library reading all those books for hours and hours at a time.

(2) Anyone at any age can make a difference.
All you need is time, the willingness to spend it and a place to sit.

There seemed to be nothing that made Greg happier than reading those books and raising that money. Until, one day, his mom took him to the theater where his godfather worked and introduced him to a whole new universe -- the world of movies.

At first, he was scared sitting in the dark theater with total strangers. But then, he became intrigued by it. Besides the backyard, the theater was the one place where he could be left without an adult to protect him, and yet, not be afraid anyone would pick on him -- after all, nobody could see him. Not that it really mattered. When the previews started playing, he forgot about everyone around him. Light, dark, crowded, empty, he could care less. The wall had come to life, and he was positively *hypnotized.*

He returned to the theater each weekend, watching the movies over and over again. And then, when he got home, he'd beg his parents to let him stay up late and watch old films playing on TV or on the VCR.

All day long, Greg imitated characters -- one minute, running up and down the stairs like he was Rocky, the boxer in *Rocky*, training for a match, and then, the next minute, pacing in front of The Silhouette Man like he was Atticus, the lawyer in *To Kill a Mockingbird*, talking to the judge.

Rose was amused by Greg's antics, but his father was not. Concerned that his son stll could not tell fiction from reality, Mark asked Greg's godfather, the one who worked at the theater, to take Greg up to the projectionist's booth, show him the machine that makes the film appear on the screen and explain how the wall doesn't *really* come to life.

Greg's godfather did as asked, but one look at the expression on the boy's face and it became clear that Mark's plan to take the magic out of movie-making not only failed -- it backfired.

The concept of one man in a little booth running the entire show left Greg even more awe-struck than the films themselves -- it was like a modern-day *Wizard of Oz*. From that day forward, he still hoped to be like the people he saw on screen, but if he never did get big enough to be like Rocky or smart enough to be like Atticus Finch, he now had a new dream to fill the void -- he was going to be the one who told their stories.

As time went on, Greg continued to insist *that* was his destiny. He was going to be the one who told the stories that played on the screen.

And not just any old stories, either. One day, he insisted, he would tell stories about underdogs just like *Rocky*, about people who stuck up for others just like *To Kill a Mockingbird*, and about places where it was okay to dream like *Willy Wonka and the Chocolate Factory*.

He said his stories would be *so* good that he would win an Academy Award for his very first one.

And night after night, while his family watched on with amusement, he got up from the dinner table, lifted up his glass like it was a trophy and practiced the first six words of his acceptance speech over and over again.

"I'd like to thank the Academy...."

**

Between the films, the books and his friends in the backyard, Greg seemed increasingly happy in his own little world -- and increasingly lost in the real one. If he had even thirty seconds to himself, his mind drifted off in a dozen different directions.

Within ten minutes of learning how to ride a ten speed bike, he got distracted, crashed, went sailing through the handle bars and cut his head wide open. On a family vacation in California, he ran through the hotel lobby and out the front door -- except that the door was closed and he went flying two feet backwards, getting a bump on the front of his head from the collision and a bump on the back from the landing.

Time and time again, he got so distracted by what was going on in his head that he literally ran nose-first right into something. (By the time he turned fifteen, he would have already cracked his head open twice and broken his nose four times -- requiring two operations.)

As time went on, Mark tried to get his son to ignore the world inside his head, but it was easier said than done. Everywhere Greg looked in the real world, there seemed to be something to fear.

Even on his own street, where all the neighbors and their kids treated him nicely, he still found plenty of excuses to be afraid. Three houses to the left, there lived a girl with pretty blue eyes. Whenever Greg saw her, he started to stutter. Three doors to the right, there lived a giant dog who always seemed like he was about to pounce. Whenever Greg saw the dog or heard it growl, he started to pee on himself.

Sometimes, Greg played catch with the boy who lived in the house next door, and other times, on weekends, he slept over at the houses of some of the other kids his age, but more often than not, he preferred to just put up a tent in his backyard and stay up late talking with his two friends, The Silhouette Man and The Ladder Horse.

At home, he just felt *safe*.

At least, he did until the burglar broke in.

One night, Greg came face-to-face with a man who broke into the house. The man ran back down the stairs and out the door as soon as he was spotted, but Greg was still trembling with fear two full hours later. His parents tried to convince him there had been no burglar -- it was just your shadow, they told him -- but it was no use. The damage was already done.

Night after night, Greg insisted on sleeping in his parents' room -- terrified that the burglar would come back to get him. When four weeks passed and he was *still* afraid to be alone, his dad decided he'd had enough. Determined to reclaim his domain, Mark surprised Greg with something that could keep him company at night -- his very own dog.

The idea worked.

Even though the eight-week-old puppy was tiny, Greg felt like he now had a "bodyguard" and finally felt safe returning to his own room.

As the days passed, Greg and the pup, who he named Tug, became practically glued at the hip. After school, they watched TV together. At dinner, Tug sat loyally by Greg's feet. At night, Tug slept on the edge of Greg's bed. There seemed to be nothing that could pull the two apart.

Over the next few months, the little puppy began to grow rapidly. In fact, by the time summer came, Tug was actually as big as Greg. And with such a big friend to protect him, Greg not only felt safe inside the house -- he finally felt safe outside of it, too. He roamed the neighborhood, smiling and happy and free -- always with his trusty companion by his side.

Until, one day, just seven months after they met, Tug was gone.

It was a Saturday afternoon in July. Greg's Little League teammates and their families were over at the house for a backyard barbeque. When one of the kids opened the front door, Tug dashed outside and ran down the street. Three blocks later, he was hit by a car and killed.

It was the first time Greg ever lost a friend to violence, and he was heartbroken. With tears streaming down his cheeks, he turned to his dad and asked him to explain how something like this could happen.

Greg's dad put his hand on his shoulder and said, "Sometimes, friends come into each other's lives, and then, when you least expect it, they move on. And there's no real explanation for it. So instead of trying to figure out why they left, all you can really do is try and appreciate them while they're here and make sure to remember them once they've gone."

Mark's comments became the basis for the third lesson of Greg's life.

(3) Approach everyone you meet like they came into your life for a reason.

The words from his father helped Greg deal with Tug's loss -- and so did the fact Tug's ashes were buried where he could keep an eye on them (in the backyard, beneath a small headstone behind three small bushes) -- but he was just not the same without his best friend by his side. Weeks turned into months, and Greg felt as sad and lonely as the day Tug died.

Hoping that some time away from home would help their son put the tragedy behind him, Rose and Mark signed Greg up for overnight camp in Wisconsin. His pal, Charlie, was signed up by his parents, too.

At first, as they boarded the bus, even with Charlie there, Greg was afraid to spend eight weeks away from home with so many strangers.

After just a few days, though, he decided summer camp in Wisconsin was just about the greatest place ever. The boy from the white picket fence suburbs was clearly no outdoorsman, but the chance to shoot a bow and arrow, run in the woods and swim in the lake was the closest thing he'd ever experienced to the adventurous world inside his head.

He also appreciated that most everyone there went out of their way to treat him nicely. Even though Greg was different (and *never* seemed to stop talking), the other kids in his cabin tried to make him feel like part of the group. The counselors were supportive, too. When Greg was nervous about trying new things, they were always there to encourage him.

The Camp Director was especially thoughtful. When he heard about Greg's eating habits, he made sure there was always a cheese sandwich waiting, just in case his finicky camper didn't eat what was being served. And when Mark sent up a box of weight-gain powder to mix in his skinny son's shakes, the Director let Greg drink the shakes in his office, so he didn't have to feel self-conscious about it in front of the other kids.

At a party with a girls' camp, Greg even got his first kiss.

He would return to Wisconsin every summer until he could drive.

When Greg returned home that first year, his parents were thrilled. Their son was finally going outside again and playing with his friends again. He even started rambling on and on about his dreams again.

Knowing how easily he got distracted, his Grandma encouraged him to start writing down those dreams on paper so he wouldn't forget them.

And so, that's exactly what he did.

When a dream crossed his mind, he wrote it down. And then, one day, he picked the ideas he cared about most and put them in a list. He entitled it *My Idea List: The First Thirty*. It was the thirty goals he hoped to reach by the time he was thirty years old.

The First Thirty included many of the typical dreams for a boy who was Greg's age. He wanted to go on a date with the blue-eyed girl three doors down. He dreamed of writing a best-selling book and winning his first argument in the Supreme Court. He also wanted to play for the Chicago Cubs and the Dallas Cowboys and be President of the United States (which he later changed to just 'live in the White House' once he remembered you can't run the country until you're 35). And somewhere along the way, he also hoped to travel to all the continents and work for the World Wrestling Federation. And on and on his "Idea List" went.

He even took the time to list the goals alphabetically, so it was only a coincidence the first one happened to be the one he cared about most:

An Academy Award for his first film

Greg's parents were not surprised by the list of wide-eyed dreams that their son put together. Most of them were things he'd been talking about (and talking about, and talking about) for years.

They knew, of course, that most of the goals were *so* big that he would probably never reach them -- at least not any time soon. But mixed in with the dreams about scoring for the Cowboys and working in the Oval Office, there was one goal on the list that seemed a lot more immediate and at least *a little* more reachable: *Going to the Ivy Leagues for college.*

Mind you, Greg didn't actually know anything about the schools that were in the elite group. He didn't know about the kind of classes they offered, or the professors who taught there, or what their campuses looked like. He couldn't even tell you exactly where they were located.

And he didn't care, either.

In fact, he didn't even care if a school was actually *in* the Ivy Leagues -- just so long as it had an 'Ivy League-ish' reputation for only admitting the 'really smart' kids. That was all he cared about.

Well, actually, he did have a second concern. *Could he get in?* Deep down, Greg didn't think he was smart enough to get into The League.

Then, one day, he saw a movie that changed *everything.*

In the film, a kid named Joel was accepted to Princeton despite getting caught breaking the law by one of the school's representatives.

Once he saw that, Greg became *certain* he could get in, too. After all, Joel *committed a crime.* Just about the worst thing Greg had ever done was put his feet on his Grandma's couch. How could he *not* get in?

He seemed to have a good point, except that *Joel didn't actually exist.* The guy was just a made-up character in a made-up movie. Of course, there was no telling Greg that. He still didn't understand -- or just didn't care -- that there was a difference between what was real and what was not.

Over the next few years, Greg began pursuing the thirty goals that he called *The First Thirty*, but most of the goals he set were *such* grand ones that he fell flat on his face trying to reach them. A part of him wanted to rip up the list like it never existed, but his Grandma urged him not to.

"Don't you remember anything I ever taught you?" Greg's Grandma scolded him, "It's okay to get knocked down once in a while. If life was nothing but straight lines, it wouldn't be worth living."

It was an important lesson to remember, and the timing could not have been better -- because Greg was about to face his toughest challenge yet.

High school.

**

From the start, Mortimer Dowhill was a struggle for Greg -- and, for the most part, he had only himself to blame.

The teachers were great, and they assured him he was doing well, but he never seemed willing to believe them -- working himself into a panic over each and every assignment. The progress reports to his parents almost always said the same thing.

"Your son is a gifted student. I just wish *he* realized it."

Outside of class, he had his share of problems, too.

As one of MDCR's only Jewish students, Greg endured anti-Semitic remarks for the first time. It only happened a few times -- just a glimpse of what people who deal with intolerance on a daily basis must face -- but as far as he was concerned, even one comment like that was one too many.

Convinced that he was too puny to make the remarks stop, Greg figured the only real solution was to just try and avoid the guys making them whenever possible -- until his Grandma stepped in.

She said, "Some of those fellas are probably just repeating what they heard other people say and have no idea what those words mean. So, they're probably not bad kids -- just stupid. So you go talk to them and explain how offensive those words are and if any of them will actually listen to you, then maybe they just might stop."

Greg reluctantly did as instructed -- asking the guys if he could sit down and talk to them. As his Grandma predicted, they mostly ignored his request, but one guy did listen to what Greg had to say and confessed that he had no idea what he was saying was as hurtful as it was. Now that someone explained it, he quickly promised to stop.

After hearing how it turned out, Greg's Grandma nodded approvingly and said, "Maybe, only one guy stopped, but the one who did, he isn't gonna just stop calling you those names. I'll bet you he won't call anybody else those names in the future, either."

(4) If you treat intolerance as hatred and avoid it, you may be less likely to endure it again. If you treat it as ignorance and address it, others may be less likely to endure it all.

By the end of the year, things at school got a whole lot better for Greg.

Sure, there were upsetting moments like the anti-Semitic remarks, but over the course of nine months, he found that the benefits of having so many diverse classmates were well worth the discomfort caused by an isolated one or two of them.

He was doing well academically, too. Despite his early self-doubts, he had continued to work hard and was ranked number one in the entire class.

Away from the textbooks, he was pursuing his interest in writing through the school newspaper and its literary magazine. He also had joined the cross country, baseball and basketball teams and was even elected Vice President of the class.

Everything seemed to be going smoothly, but it did not take long for him to hit another roadblock -- *literally.*

All summer, he worked as a busboy to earn enough money to buy a car (his father had agreed to match one dollar for every dollar he earned).

In the fall, when he turned sixteen, he got his license and started showing off his brand new automobile all over town. Two days later, he got in a horrible accident and the front of the car went up in flames.

Working and working to reach a goal, only to come crashing to the ground just as he was starting to celebrate his success -- it would be a metaphor for the story of Greg's life.

*(5) No matter how far you've come,
always keep your eyes focused on the road ahead.*

The crash was not the only setback during his second year at MDCR.

One weekend, Greg found himself in a neighborhood where he'd never been and was beat up. The people who did it happened to be minorities, and there were some who said the attack was a reflection on *all* minorities. The remarks upset Greg almost as much as the incident itself.

Racially-charged issues can be very complex, but as far as he was concerned, this one was pretty straightforward. *It made no sense.* How can the actions of a single person tell you something about other people just because they happen to have the same color skin?

As Greg told one friend, "If a guy with dark hair does something bad, it doesn't mean all guys with dark hair are bad. So if it's a guy with dark skin, why would it be any different?"

In the weeks that followed, one small positive thing did come out of the unfortunate event. Greg *finally* started going to the gym. His dad had been urging him to lift weights for quite some time, and Greg did want to get bigger, but he was *so* skinny that he always had been afraid that he'd get laughed out of the weight room if he ever dared step inside. After getting beat up, though, he no longer cared whether he was going to get teased at the gym. This was about self-defense. He *needed* to get bigger in case he ever had to protect himself.

As it turned out, once he did go to the gym, nobody there laughed at all. In fact, most of the big guys went out of their way to help him. They taught him how to use the weights and offered words of encouragement.

When Greg admitted to one of them he was surprised by how nicely they treated a skinny kid just getting started, one of the bodybuilder types patted him on the back and said, "We all started somewhere."

(6) Whether it's people or places, you need to look beyond the surface
if you really want to know what they're like inside.

Greg was excited to have a new circle of friends from the gym, but he still couldn't stop thinking of the assault that led him there in the first place. From his perspective, it was another example that proved he had to overcome more setbacks than most -- that his life just wasn't *fair*.

Mark had mixed emotions about the situation. On the one hand, he felt badly Greg faced so many hurdles. On the other hand, he took it as a personal insult when his pampered son complained about his 'tough' life.

Mark said, "Sure, Greg faced setbacks, but there were kids whose lives were a thousand times tougher than his. I provided a good life for him, and I felt it was time he realized that. That's why I introduced him to Kahzti."

Kahzti grew up in an unsafe part of the world. At a young age, he left home to come to America. When he arrived -- a teenager in a foreign land -- Kahzti had no family, no money and didn't know the language. Yet, he managed to scrape up enough money to get by, learn English *and* finish high school ranked at the top of his class.

Mark heard about Kahzti and had such respect for him that he quietly cut a check to help pay for him to go to college. And now, Mark hoped that Kahzti would repay the gift by giving Greg a check -- *a reality check.*

The idea worked.

After meeting the soft-spoken, humble young man and hearing about his struggles, Greg realized how small his own obstacles actually were.

(7) The best way to put your problems in perspective is to spend time
with someone who can only dream their life was so easy.

Greg returned to school in the fall more determined than ever to reach his goals. And by year's end, in and out of class, he was *thriving*.

He was an appointed Student Leader, a varsity athlete, elected twice to class office, an editor for the school paper and editor-in-chief of the literary magazine. In his free time, he lifted weights and coached a team in the Little League he played in as a boy. And other than Art (he still couldn't draw), his GPA was nearly perfect.

In his mind, the Ivy Leagues had gone from a total fantasy to a virtual certainty, but the lessons of the past few summers remained with him -- so, instead of slacking off, Greg swore he would stay even more focused and work even harder -- using his final year of high school as a chance to test himself and try new things he had never done before.

One of those challenges he vowed to tackle was varsity football.

He used to be so scrawny that his bones practically poked through his skin, but after drinking all those shakes with the weight-gain powder, spending all those hours in the gym and finally eating regular foods, he had filled out his six foot frame. And now, the boy who once ran around the yard pretending he was on the Cowboys wanted to play *for real*.

So, a few weeks before his senior year, to get ready for the upcoming season, Greg took an all-day bus ride to Knox to attend a four day football camp with hundreds of other players from dozens of other high schools around the country. Despite his fond memories of summers in Wisconsin, Greg was nervous as he boarded the bus -- but once again, camp turned out to be as much fun as anything he'd ever done.

On the field, he proved to be a quick study -- named one of the camp's all-stars during closing ceremonies. Off the field, he made a new friend. A kid named Bailey. On the surface, the two boys seemed very different, but that's all most of their differences were -- *on the surface*.

Despite coming from different races and backgrounds, they actually had a lot in common. The two hit it off right away and stayed in touch even after camp ended. It seemed to be the beginning of a great, new friendship.

For Greg, the season itself got off to a great start, too.

He scored a touchdown in his first game and a 90 yard TD in his second. And while the team didn't win any championships, just being a part of it felt like a victory for a kid who used to be teased about his size.

By December, he was feeling on top of the world. He was just one semester shy of graduation, his college applications had all been sent in and, the way he saw it, his road to a prosperous future was set in stone.

He packed his bags for winter vacation, convinced that he had finally navigated his way through the rough waters of life. Little did he know, the smooth sailing was just the calm before the storm.

**

The tempest began on Greg's very first day back at school after the holidays, when a classmate delivered some terrible news. While Greg was out of town, his buddy from football camp, Bailey, was shot and killed -- an innocent victim of a drive-by shooting.

Greg was overwhelmed when he heard about what had happened.

Make no mistake, it wasn't that he lost a *lifelong* friend -- the two only spent a few days together -- but in a sense, *that* was what struck him most. The fact that, while he thought he made a new good friend -- and still did -- he really didn't know much about Bailey at all. When they were together, Greg had simply never felt any sense of urgency to learn much about him. He just kind of assumed that was what the next seventy years were for.

His dad actually taught him otherwise when he was little -- when Tug was killed -- but Greg obviously lost sight of that lesson over the years -- making it all the more painful to have to learn again.

A few weeks later, hoping it would brighten Greg's spirits, his mom gave him pictures from their vacation, but it actually made things worse.

In his heart, Greg knew the pictures didn't tell the *whole* story -- how he spent much of the trip complaining about having to share a hotel room with his sister and a dozen other things that were so clearly unimportant now that he knew how those same days turned out for Bailey.

It was a stark contrast that Greg would think about for years to come. But, in the meantime, he still had a final semester of high school to get through -- and his own nightmare was just beginning.

For most high school seniors, spring is a time of great anxiety -- when they find out if they've been accepted to the universities of their dreams. For Greg, it was a time of *anticipation*. He applied to a handful of the nation's most esteemed schools, and he expected to get in to all of them.

He could hardly contain his excitement about the road ahead. His old friend, Charlie, was going to the Ivy Leagues (Harvard Charlie, people had started calling him) and everyone thought he was brilliant because of it -- and Greg felt certain he would be looked at the same way once he was accepted. He was actually going to be *one of them.*

Or so he thought.

One by one, the responses from the schools began to arrive in Greg's mailbox, and they all seemed to say the same thing.

No.

In the end, Greg was rejected from every college he wanted to attend.

His fast track to success had been *completely derailed* and he had no idea why. He'd worked so hard and achieved so much that it just did not seem possible. He called each school, desperately hoping there had been a mistake, but they insisted there'd been none. He felt like the world was collapsing around him -- and yet, things were about to get even worse.

After the rejections arrived, Greg paid a visit to Avery Welton.

A few months earlier, during the application process, Greg asked Mr. Welton to write a recommendation letter for him. Welton eventually agreed to do it, but only after first saying he did not want to because he did not think an Ivy League level school was the right fit for Greg. Now that the schools replied -- and apparently agreed with Welton -- Greg hoped Welton could help him make sense of it all.

Welton told Greg there was no way to know for certain what tipped the scales against him, but he said he did have an idea what might have done it. And it was then that Welton gave him a copy of the "recommendation" letter. As he read it, Greg went from confused to *crushed.*

The letter did say he was hard-working and succeeded at most every-thing he tried -- but that praise was weaved within a web of criticism and ridicule. In the "recommendation" letter, Welton claimed Greg had poor diction, little charm and asked questions that suggested he had no idea what was going on. He mocked Greg's interest in poetry. Welton even wrote that Greg, who was being recruited by some of the colleges for sports, had a complete minimum of athletic talent.

The words would have hurt coming from anyone at any time. But to come from someone he looked up to so much? In a letter that could impact the rest of his life? Greg didn't know whether to scream or cry.

When pressed for an explanation, Welton insisted he did it for the kid's own good. When Greg refused to heed his advice to lower his dreams and went ahead and applied to Ivy League-level schools, Welton said he took the matter into his own hands -- writing a letter of "recommendation" actually designed to hurt Greg's chances of getting in. He said he knew Greg and his family would be upset when they first saw the letter, but he insisted that in the long run, he had done them a favor because Greg just didn't have the brains to cut it at such elite schools.

No matter how Welton justified his action, there was no denying the personal impact it had on Greg. He was *crushed.*

Charlie said, "He wasn't angry as much as he was just really *down.* It reminded me of how he was when we were younger and his dog died."

Greg's Grandma didn't like what she was seeing.

She said, "How many times have I said not to dwell on life being full of curves? You gotta get up, dust yourself off and keep going."

In the end, as always, Greg's Grandma won out.

(8) Never let failure keep you from trying again.

Greg started to try and pick up the pieces by contacting the colleges he wanted to attend and urging them to reconsider. When none would reverse their decision, he swallowed his pride and began calling other schools -- some he had never even heard of -- *begging* them to give him a chance.

Until, finally, mercifully, he found a school that would take him.

A school located in... *Louisiana???*

**

In the fall, Greg boarded a plane with his bags by his side and a chip on his shoulder. After what he'd just been through, part of him was happy to escape to a place where he didn't know anyone, but he had never been to Louisiana or any place like it and had no real desire to be there now.

He also had no intention of staying long.

Night after night, he stayed up late studying for his classes -- so he could get the grades he needed to "get back on track" and transfer to one of the schools where he was "supposed to go."

When he wasn't studying for his own classes, he was helping kids at a local grade school study for theirs. He saw each kid he helped -- each kid he encouraged to chase a dream -- as a chance to turn the negative in his life into a positive in someone else's. And, at the very least, it was a great distraction. Every minute spent helping those kids was a minute not spent dwelling on the detour his life had taken.

Between classes, homework, volunteering and his daily visits to the gym, Greg's schedule had quickly filled up. And yet, there was still one thing clearly missing. *Friends.*

While his classmates were getting to know each other and enjoying the freedom college brings, the Ivy League reject was acting more like a wrongly imprisoned man. He even went so far as to hang up a Martin Luther King, Jr. poster outside his door, pull his mattress into the hall and stage his own little version of a sit-in -- convinced he had been denied his "constitutional right" to attend the college of his choice.

And then, one day, he met a classmate from Texas named Galloway who had a point of view unlike any he'd ever heard. She was accepted to the Ivy Leagues but chose Louisiana instead. When Greg asked her why, Galloway said she simply picked the school she thought was better.

Greg didn't want to be rude, but this was just about the craziest thing he ever heard and he felt like he had to say something.

The girl from Texas listened to him politely and then said, "Look, just because we didn't have the same dream doesn't mean one of us is wrong. It just means our dreams were different. The Ivy Leagues *are* good schools, but so is this one. And if you opened your mind a little and gave the place a chance, you just might see why so many of us like it here."

It was a statement Greg sorely needed to hear. In the weeks that followed, he began making more of an effort to meet his classmates and become involved on campus. In the process, he discovered just how right Galloway had been about what he'd find if he gave the place a chance.

(9) Respect the goals and dreams of others as if they were your own.

As it turned out, that conversation was just one of several events over the next several months that made Greg stop and think. His first semester of college also was an election season, and it was certainly no ordinary one. Of the two men trying to become the next governor of Louisiana, one was an alleged racist and the other had a long history of alleged corruption.

The election brought the issues of race, ethnicity and abuse of power front and center -- and it would not be the only time.

During that same period, Native American groups around the country were protesting against a number of sports teams. They said the teams' names and mascots degraded Native American culture and history. The teams responded by insisting the names and mascots were a 'tribute' -- that the Native American groups were being overly sensitive.

The protestors had voiced their feelings in the past, but with the Braves in the World Series, the debate was in the spotlight like rarely before.

And then, there were the L.A. riots.

A group of white policemen were accused of beating up an unarmed black man. A jury found them not guilty, despite the fact the incident was caught on video. After the jury's decision was announced, riots broke out around Los Angeles. But even before the verdict and its violent aftermath, the videotaped beating and the reaction to it demonstrated that our nation was still a very divided one.

With all of these events taking place, Greg began paying more and more attention to the racial climate around him.

In the process, he found that there didn't seem to be any tension between students of different backgrounds on his campus -- everybody seemed to get along fine -- but in many cases, there didn't seem to be much interaction, either. The groups seemed to be *co-existing side by side* instead of *co-existing together.*

And nowhere was that more clear than it was by The Benches.

In the middle of campus, there were two sets of benches just a few feet apart. Every day, dozens if not hundreds of students spent time there in between classes -- catching up with friends about the events of the day. And every afternoon, almost without fail, the white students hung out by one set of benches. The black students hung out by the other.

The separation was completely voluntary -- it wasn't like there were signs "Whites Only" and "Blacks Only" -- but it happened all the same. Black kids sat over here, white kids sat over there, and few if any ever crossed the imaginary line between them.

The situation bothered Greg a great deal

It wasn't that he thought there was anything wrong with people having friends from the same background. (And make no mistake, he was no different. Day after day, he visited The Benches and sat with the students who looked like him.) It was just that he figured everyone's lives would be that much more interesting if they expanded their circle of friends. So, he couldn't understand why nobody, himself included, ever seemed to take that first step toward bridging the gap between the two groups.

As the days passed, the questions continued to swirl around his head.

How can the choices for Governor come down to a man who appears to be corrupt and one who appears to be racist?

Why are so many white people shocked by the videotaped assault of an unarmed black man by some white cops when so many black people say the only thing that is surprising is the fact it was caught on tape?

If the names and mascots that appear to stereotype Native Americans really are a 'tribute' to their culture like the teams claim, then why aren't there teams with names like 'Blacks', 'Hispanics', and 'Jews'?

How come students seem to divide into groups based on their race when they sit by The Benches? Why doesn't anyone ever seem to bridge that gap? Wouldn't they all understand each other better if someone did?

With all of these questions running through his mind, Greg became more interested than ever in exploring issues like intolerance, diversity and discrimination. He signed up for courses such as Civil Rights, History of Anti-Semitism and Race & Gender, and he began writing research papers on the use of stereotypes in the media and racial bias in the justice system.

In the process, his own sense of being "denied a constitutional right" was put back into proper perspective -- obviously, he had not been denied any at all -- and the image of Martin Luther King, Jr. outside his door took on a whole new meaning. Instead of seeing the poster as a symbol of what he *personally* endured, he began to see it as a symbol of what one man could do to address what *others* endure. A symbol of what one man could do to bring people of different races and backgrounds together. What one man could do to build a bridge where none exists.

The more Greg thought about that, the less he thought about his own problems and the more he began to think about problems faced by others.

And it was right then and there, sitting on a mattress in the middle of Louisiana, with the poster of Dr. King looking over his shoulder, that a no-shoe-wearing, cereal-straight-out-of-the-box-eating, milkshake-drinking, Ivy League reject began to hatch a *Dream* of his own.

It would be years until Greg pursued his *Dream* -- or revealed what it was, or even that he had one -- but, in the meantime, he began increasing his civic efforts by recruiting his classmates to come volunteer with him at a grade school just a few blocks away. He also joined the campus group for students interested in community service.

Then, in the summer, he worked for a U.S. Senator. For Greg, the internship was a powerful introduction to the good side of public service. The Senator was a true public servant -- serving in the military before coming to Capitol Hill. His staff was inspiring, too -- working long hours day after day to try and help the citizens back home.

Not surprisingly, Greg's stint in D.C. was also marked by a number of memorable adventures. On one occasion, he went to the White House to visit with an intern he'd met a few days earlier -- and somehow managed to find himself at a podium reading off announcements to military officials. On another occasion, while attending the Presidential Convention in New York, Greg was asked to help out by going on stage and checking the microphone. He did as asked, except that, instead of saying 'Testing 1-2-3', he delivered a full-fledged speech like *he* was the guy running for office.

A staffer later laughed, "You gotta realize, this was going on in the morning before the Convention actually started, so the kid was giving his 'speech' to a sound check guy and about 15,000 empty seats."

The summer spent in D.C. motivated Greg to expand his civic efforts when he returned to college in the fall. Instead of just volunteering in the community, he began "bringing the community to campus" as well -- arranging for the kids he tutored to come sit in his college classes, attend basketball games and meet his other classmates and professors. The idea was popular -- even the Dean volunteered his time to be part of it.

By the end of his sophomore year, Greg had come a long way.

Academically, he had excelled -- an A in every single course he'd taken. His efforts to encourage others to volunteer had led the Dean to appoint him Chairman of Community Service for the whole college. Socially, considering his rocky start, he'd come a long way, too. He had been elected twice to class office and even joined a fraternity.

The fraternity house played host to fun times, but it also was a place where a lot of valuable lessons were learned. Of all the ones Greg learned, the one he needed most was taught to him by a guy named Eric Winger.

Nicknamed 'Juice' for his orange hair, Eric was just about the funniest person Greg ever met. At least, that's what Greg thought until he started to realize that Juice's one-liners always seemed to be about *him*. Still as sensitive as ever, Greg angrily demanded Juice stop making fun of him.

"You gotta lighten up, you know that?" the easy-going Southerner said with a laugh. "I'm not making fun of you. I'm just cracking jokes."

Greg said he wasn't so sure he understood the difference.

Juice replied, "Nobody else is here but us when I tell them."

It was true. In front of others, Juice never made fun of his friends. The jokes only started when they were hanging out by themselves.

(10) You can usually tell the difference between joking and teasing by counting the number of people around to hear the punch line.

As much as he would've never dreamed it possible when he first stepped off that plane two years earlier, Greg had come to like life in the Deep South. There were foods he'd never tried, music he'd never heard and a down-home hospitality he'd never experienced.

And yet, as much as he liked it, there was still one thing missing. Something that always lingered in the back of his mind. For all the things Louisiana was, there was one thing it wasn't and never would be.

The Ivy Leagues.

No matter how much Greg liked Louisiana, he still wished for a chance to prove he could succeed at the schools that rejected him.

And so, he decided to stick to his original plan and transfer in the fall.

The Dean insisted he was making a *huge* mistake. He said that Greg was doing so well in Louisiana that he should really think twice before giving it all up just for the chance to start over at some other school.

"It's not *some other school*," Greg insisted. "It's *the Ivy Leagues*."

The Dean held firm, reminding him that the grass isn't always greener on the other side -- but his advice was falling on deaf ears. Greg's mind was made up, and it seemed like nothing was going to change it. And then, the Dean told him about Junior Year Abroad -- the program that lets college students spend up to two semesters studying in another country.

Other than a short trip to Israel when he was a boy, Greg had never crossed the ocean and was intrigued by the idea of going overseas.

"What do the students study when they're in the program?" he asked.

The Dean explained that was the best part of all. Depending on where a student chose to go, there was a wide range of subjects he or she could study -- from how to speak another language to how to make movies.

Greg had already learned another language (Spanish), but the moment he heard those four magic words -- *how to make movies* -- he lit up like a Christmas tree. The thought of reaching Goal #1 from *The First Thirty* -- winning an Academy Award for his first film -- began dancing around his head. Quicker than you can say *quiet on the set!*, Greg scrapped the plan that seemed so set in stone just a few moments earlier. Instead of seeking a transfer to the Ivy Leagues, he decided he would spend his junior year in Europe learning about filmmaking and then come back to Louisiana to wrap up college and get his degree.

When summer arrived, Greg went home with a sense of excitement about the road ahead and the trip to Europe in the fall. But just like when he was little, with time on his hands, his mind began to wander. So, as the summer wound down, second thoughts started creeping into his head. Was the trip abroad *really* about learning to make films? Or was it just a way to avoid finding out if he actually could cut it in the Ivy Leagues?

His mother urged him to let those doubts go -- to focus his energy on the future instead of thinking about what might have been.

Her words made sense, but in the heat of the moment, they made Greg furious. He became convinced that what she was *really* trying to say was she didn't think he was smart enough for the Ivy Leagues.

He stormed out of the house and went for a drive to calm down. He intended to go see his Grandma, but really wasn't paying much attention, and, as always, he got lost. A left turn here, a u-turn there, and before Greg knew it, he was driving through Vernon Froehmann Whitfield University.

Since it wasn't on the East Coast, Froehmann Whitfield was not part of the Ivy Leagues, but it might as well have been. By all accounts, it was one of the most highly regarded universities in the nation.

As Greg sat in his car and watched the students walk past, smiling and happy, wearing t-shirts and shorts and hats with the school's name and colors, he became consumed with jealousy. He knew the students walking down the sidewalk were all probably much brighter than he was, but he refused to believe they were *better*. In his heart, Greg knew he would have outworked them all if only he'd been given the chance.

He knew he should just go back home and stop dwelling on it, but now that he was this close, he just could not walk away. He had to know, if only for a few seconds, what it was like to be *one of them*.

He got out of his car and slipped into the crowd of students. He only meant to walk a couple feet, but with each step, he became more and more convinced he fit in and it became harder and harder to walk away.

He *was* one of them. And once and for all, he was going to prove it.

His heart racing, his confidence growing with every step, he veered off the sidewalk, into a school office and declared he was there to enroll.

When he got home a few hours later, his mom was sitting in the kitchen. When he walked in, she asked, "Where have you been all day?"

"Vernon Froehmann Whitfield University," he said.

"Visiting friends?" she asked.

"No," he said, with tears in his eyes. "I go there now."

(11) No matter the odds against you, they always improve if you show up.

As impossible as it seemed, he had shown up unannounced at one of the nation's top universities, decided on the spot he wanted to go there and literally talked his way in.

Well, sort of.

In fact, he struck something of a deal. He was going to get to attend classes for one year just like the "real" students, and get grades in those classes just like the "real" students. If he did well, he could stay. If he didn't do well, he'd have to leave -- and there wouldn't be any refund.

For the school, there really was nothing to lose.

For Greg, on the other hand, his entire future was at risk -- but it was a gamble he felt he had to take. He wanted to prove he never should have been rejected from all those schools three years earlier. He wanted to prove Mr. Welton was wrong. He wanted to prove, once and for all, he was good enough to be *one of them*. And, he felt, if he could succeed at a school with such a top-flight reputation, he would finally do just that.

**

Vernon Froehmann Whitfield University seemed to have everything a student could want -- brilliant professors, interesting courses, talented classmates, a beautiful campus -- but for Greg, the opportunity to go there came at a very steep price.

Just as his old Dean warned, he was like a freshman starting from scratch. In the blink of an eye, Greg had gone from being a big fish to feeling hopelessly lost at sea. Just finding his way to class was a challenge, never mind the assignments already piling up on his lap.

And it wasn't just the workload weighing him down.

Within days of setting foot on campus, Greg began to butt heads with the people in charge at Froehmann Whitfield.

His mom, Rose, recalled, "Shortly after he started going to classes, he requested a meeting with a school official and was told he would have to make an appointment, and he wasn't too happy about that."

Clearly, it was unreasonable for Greg to expect someone overseeing thousands of students to meet with him at the drop of a hat, but in his defense, that level of access was all he had ever known.

Mortimer Dowhill was a small high school with an 'open door policy' that gave students the chance to talk directly with school officials with little else required besides a knock when they entered. Louisiana was obviously bigger, but Greg served in several student leadership positions so the Dean and other school officials always made time for him if it was important.

When he didn't receive the same treatment at Froehmann Whitfield, he insisted it was *personal* -- that it had to do with his 'Special Student' status.

"The lady told me to take a number," he muttered angrily. "They don't consider me a *real* student. They would *never* say that to a real student!"

He didn't fare too well off campus, either.

He got a job delivering food on weekends, but he kept getting lost and was let go after just one night.

Those old feelings -- that nobody ever believed in his abilities -- started to come back and the chip on Greg's shoulder began to grow bigger and bigger by the day. Instead of putting up the poster of Dr. King in his new room, he literally put up a giant poster of a pitbull.

He was angry, lonely and overwhelmed, but he refused to quit. He woke up early and stayed up late -- whatever it took to get his work done.

In his free time, just as in Louisiana, he used volunteering as a way to distract himself from thinking about the things that upset him. In this case, he tutored former gang members trying to get their high school degree.

He also worked out his frustration through daily visits to the gym.

Of course, nothing put him in a better mood than his Grandma. And now that he was going to college just ten minutes down the road from her apartment, he was able to see her in person on a more regular basis --

cementing the bond that was already the strongest one he had.

But that was it. Exercising, volunteering and visiting his Grandma.

Other than an occasional date or two, virtually every other waking minute was spent going to class or studying for one.

And, in the end, that tunnel vision paid off.

Despite the odds against a guy showing up out of nowhere, adjusting to a new environment and acing all his classes, that's exactly what Greg did. With an A in every course, he passed the test with flying colors and earned the right to stay at Froehmann Whitfield.

And yet, ironically enough, even after he became a "real" student, he didn't seem to fit in with his peers. Some went out of their way to try and include him in their plans, but he rarely accepted the invitations. When the other students went to eat, he stayed home to study. When they went to basketball games, he studied. When they went to parties, he studied.

It was as if he was still more interested in *proving* he should be one of them than actually *being* one of them.

To add to his troubles, Greg continued to clash with school officials.

Harvard Charlie recalled, "There were a whole list of things they did that upset him. He'd call me at least once a week with the latest. The one that comes to mind first was the thing with his credits."

When a student switches colleges, in many cases, he or she has to stay an extra semester and take a couple extra classes because the new school's requirements for graduation are slightly different than the old one's.

It was perfectly routine, but when it happened to Greg, he again became convinced he was being singled out. He started firing off angry letters demanding administrators leave him alone.

As the weeks passed and the conflicts at school continued, Greg began spending more time in the weight room to work out his frustration -- and before long, it started to show.

By the time his fifth year of college rolled around, the skinny boy afraid of the neighbor's dog was a young man bench-pressing 300 pounds. Instead of bones poking out of his chest, veins now popped out of his arms.

It seemed like he practically *exploded* into a whole new person, but there was really nothing sudden about it. Greg had been working out for years, had been drinking those weight-gain shakes for even longer, was finally eating regular foods *and* he had genetics on his side (His dad, Mark, was six foot three and over two hundred pounds). And yet, despite all of those factors, even Greg seemed shocked by his reflection.

A friend and college neighbor named Kim laughed, "He would stand in the mirror and flex over and over, but it wasn't in a look-how-tough-I-am kind of way. It was a more of a I-was-skinnier-than-a-toothpick-where-did-these-muscles-come-from kind of way. It was really pretty funny to see the expression on his face. I'd never seen him so happy."

Just like always, though, his joy was short-lived.

"Nobody changes that much," skeptics howled. "You took steroids!"

The comments were just plain dumb, but they hurt him deeply.

"It's not right!" he wailed. "They have no right to say that about me!"

Greg's Grandma had little patience for the whining.

She huffed, "Why do you care what those people say? *You* know what you did and what you didn't. That's the only thing that matters."

As always, her advice helped. He resumed his workouts, as focused as ever, and did his best to just ignore those who questioned him.

Greg's success in the weight room was outmatched only by his success in class. Five years after being told he wasn't good enough for the Ivy Leagues, and three years after walking into Vernon Froehmann Whitfield University right off the street, Greg graduated at the top of his class.

In all, he finished college with 37 A's and a B.

He had every right to feel proud of what he accomplished. Despite all the detours and all the obstacles, Greg just kept chugging along, until he got exactly where he always dreamed he would be -- the cream of the crop at an 'Ivy League level' school.

And yet, at what should've been his crowning moment, all Greg felt was *regret*. Because, for all the great things Froehmann Whitfield was, there was one thing missing -- one thing it wasn't and never would be.

Louisiana.

After three long years, Greg missed his friends, his professors and the Dean. He missed the kids at the school where he volunteered and all his fraternity brothers, to whom he'd never properly said goodbye. He also missed the weather, the culture, the music and the Southern hospitality.

Having been at Froehmann Whitfield for three years, he understood why so many kids thought it was an amazing college and wanted to go there -- but *he* had gone there for the wrong reason...and he knew it.

For more than four years, he insisted that "recommendation" letter could not define who he was or what he could achieve. And yet, he gave up what he loved in Louisiana -- not to mention, the plan to study film in Europe -- all just for the chance to get a diploma with a name on it that he thought would impress people more. The kid who insisted he should not be measured by a piece of paper sacrificed everything for...a piece of paper.

And now, that's all his diploma seemed like -- a piece of paper. Instead of symbolizing the success he achieved at Froehmann Whitfield, it served only as a painful reminder of what he gave up -- and endured -- to be there.

He felt *so* strongly about it that he said he never wanted to see the diploma a single time and said he would not even attend the graduation ceremony where the degrees were handed out.

His Grandma was *furious*. She said not going to the ceremony was like not crossing the finish line in a marathon.

"And what about me?" she growled. "I've got pictures of all my other grandkids in their caps and gowns. You *have* to go to that ceremony."

Despite how strongly she felt, Greg defied her orders -- offering her little more than an empty promise that somehow, some day, he'd get her a picture of him in a cap and gown.

His parents, surprisingly enough, didn't seem too upset. Watching their son cross the stage would have been nice, but they were too happy with his grades to put up much of a fight. As one of Froehmann Whitfield's top graduates, he had his pick where to go next -- whether it was an elite law school or a high-paying corporate job, whichever his heart desired.

And that was when his parents found out he no longer desired either.

Despite his degree and the honors that came with it, Greg told his parents he would not be interviewing with any company for any position -- and he wouldn't be applying to any law school, either. He told them his up-and-down road the last few years had caused him to reconsider his future, his purpose and what it really meant to be a success.

Simply put, in the process of getting back on the fast track to corporate America, he found a place he'd rather be -- in a school, working with kids who are overlooked and underestimated like he had been.

"And that," he explained to his parents, "is why I've decided to set all my old goals on hold and spend one year substitute teaching."

His parents were absolutely stunned.

Mark said, "Teaching is a fine profession -- just not for Greg. He didn't know the first thing about it. And what's more, with the grades he just got, there was a pot of gold waiting for him in corporate America. So, the whole idea was crazy. Not that I was surprised. This is a kid who ran into walls."

Hoping some time in the sun would bring his oldest child to his senses, Mark gave Greg a ticket to California as his graduation gift.

The plan almost worked. The chance to be near Hollywood did cause Greg to think once again about pursuing his lifelong wish to write stories and make movies, but he just couldn't get teaching out of his head.

He knew it was a far cry from the path most kids in his position choose to follow. It certainly wasn't going to bring him a salary like the one Harvard Charlie was getting from the multi-billion dollar global consulting firm that hired him after graduation -- but this was the direction Greg wanted to go. He wanted to spend one year working with kids who were frequently underestimated, and he wanted to do it now rather than later.

So, he packed up his bags and headed home.

"Maybe, one day I'll go back to California," Greg told his mom and dad. "Maybe, one day I'll go to law school. Maybe, one day I'll join corporate America. But none of those one days are today. Today, I've gotta follow my heart, and my heart's telling me to be a substitute teacher."

**

In preparation for his new job, Greg moved into a small apartment in the city -- an apartment whose window happened to overlook the very neighborhood where he expected to work as a substitute teacher.

While he waited for the call to get started, Greg decided to put the extra free time to use by trying yet again to learn the skill that eluded him all his life -- how to draw. This time, he decided, he'd teach himself.

Harvard Charlie laughed loudly when he heard the idea.

"How can you teach yourself something you don't know?"

Charlie did seem to have a point, and in fact, Greg's new sketches were just as bad as the ones he drew when he was little. But he stuck with it -- spending hours and hours on each drawing -- and somehow, they actually started to improve. They still weren't *good*, but they were good enough to motivate Greg to keep working at it on a daily basis.

To fill the rest of his time, he started helping his dad with finance work during the week, kept lifting weights at the gym in the evenings and began working at a new restaurant/bar called The Club on the weekends.

The Club was a real classy, upscale place that quickly became *the place to be* for top executives (and had a line down the street to prove it).

Greg's job was an easy one -- he stood by the door, greeted customers and checked the bathroom once an hour to make sure it was clean. But just like always, there were bumps in the road.

He was fired after one night.

It was the result of a misunderstanding -- The Boss thought Greg took ten dollars he wasn't supposed to take -- but it hardly seemed worth fighting over. The job only paid a few bucks an hour, he'd only worked there one night, and he was planning on quitting once he began substitute teaching.

The logical thing was to just walk away, but Greg refused to do it until he wrote a note to The Boss to try and clear things up.

Within hours of getting the note, The Boss realized a mistake probably had been made, called to apologize and even offered Greg the job back.

Greg was stunned by the call. He never expected The Boss to call up and admit it was a misunderstanding. When The Boss did, Greg was deeply impressed. He knew this was someone he could learn from. So much so, he immediately accepted the job back and even decided he would keep working there on weekends after he started substitute teaching.

> *(12) If you come across someone you can learn from,*
> *make the effort to be around them as much as you can.*

On his first day as a sub, Greg was assigned to Blue Academy in a section of the city known as The Green.

Greg had never before stepped foot in The Green, but he'd certainly heard of it. All his life, in fact, he saw the stories in the paper and on TV. Stories about drugs and violence and despair. He'd also heard that white people were not too welcome there.

At one point, those myths might have been enough to cause him to stay as far away as possible, but after the big guys in the weight room and his classmates in Louisiana both showed him how wrong assumptions can be, he knew not to pre-judge a place where he had never been.

And so it was, on a cold January morning, that a twenty-four year old part-time restaurant doorman strolled out his door, past the train tracks and into The Green for his first day as a substitute teacher.

As it turned out, Greg did have problems that first day in The Green -- but it had nothing to do with the neighborhood. It had to do with teaching.
He didn't know how.

That first day, after being greeted graciously by Principal Brooks and his warm-hearted clerk, Ms. Boggs, inside Blue Academy's front door, Greg was given a room number and sent on his way. He assumed it was the room where he would be trained -- but when he walked in, it was an *actual* class with *actual* students expecting him to teach them something.

The kids behaved fine, but Greg quickly found himself overwhelmed -- the day, a complete disaster. In the weeks that followed, the job didn't get much easier -- as he found out the hard way that knowing something and actually being able to *teach* it were two different things (especially while monitoring twenty or twenty-five students at once).

The experience frustrated Greg to no end. The full-time teachers made it look so effortless -- like jugglers gracefully tossing around six bowling pins at once with their eyes closed -- but when he tried to step in their place and do it, he always seemed to drop everything.

Night after night, Greg stayed awake, staring out the window, wishing he could be as good as the full-time teachers. Until finally, one time, tired of his sleepless nights, he literally threw out his bed.

It would be seven long months until he got a new one.

On the bright side, there was one thing Greg did do well -- *names*. He could memorize an entire class full of them in minutes. The kids seemed amazed he could do it, but more than anything, they wondered why he bothered. After all, he was a sub. It's not like he'd be with them all year.

He always responded the same way -- telling them that whether he was there for one day or forever, he still wanted to know them as individuals instead of assuming they were all the same.

"And the first step in doing that," he told them, "is knowing your names because names are the first thing that set us apart from each other."

It was a saying he repeated so often that one kid even drew a cartoon of him saying it. And years later, that same girl sent him a note thanking him for the difference he made in her life -- a note that ended with one simple phrase: "Thank you again for knowing my name."

(13) Never underestimate the value of knowing someone's name.
A person's name is the most important word in the world.

As he got to know the students better, Greg found the biggest obstacle for some of them had little to do with confidence in themselves. It had to do with confidence in *others*. Having seen people in their community treated poorly just because of where they live or the color of their skin, some of the kids questioned whether they would get a fair shake to succeed when they got older even if they did put in the time and effort.

Searching for a way to convince them they could accomplish anything they put their mind to -- even if they had to create their own opportunity to do it -- Greg told the kids about his lifelong struggle with art. He told them how he could barely draw a straight line as a kid, and how instead of giving up, he just kept practicing. And then, he pulled out the scrapbook where he kept his sketches to show them the progress he'd been making.

A twenty-four year old man, twenty-five kids and a book of drawings. Little did anyone know that just a few weeks later that moment in time would change Greg's life -- and thousands of others -- for years to come.

*

It was a cool weekend morning, when Greg walked out his door to pick up his sister for brunch. At the very same time, two boys from Blue Academy happened to be heading down the very same street on their way to get some sodas. The moment they saw Greg, they recognized him from school (they didn't actually remember his name -- just that he was the "new guy with big ears who could draw") and hustled ahead to say hello.

After learning the boys were on their way to get sodas, Greg offered to get them milkshakes if they wanted to join him and his sister instead. The two boys quickly accepted, but Greg's sister changed her mind -- upset that her brother, as always, lost track of time and was late to pick her up.

So off they went, a white substitute teacher and two black students, to Gordon Birchwood's Terrace -- a popular, casual restaurant located in a an upscale part of town.

When the trio arrived, they were seated at a table next to a middle-aged white woman. As they sat down, the lady gave the two African-American boys a look of disdain and moved her purse to the far side of her table in a way that suggested she was afraid one of them might steal it.

Greg was *enraged*. How could she make a presumption about two kids she never met? As far as he was concerned, it just made no sense.

He was tempted to say that right to her face, but he never uttered a single word in her direction. Rather than worry about what she thought, he decided to just use the negative moment as an excuse to do something positive. So, he rose from his seat, approached the head of the restaurant, and said, "Do you see those two kids? I'm coming back with *ten*."

Initially, as people heard about the incident, most presumed that the customer was obviously triggered by her stereotypes about minorities. But in later years, as Greg's civic efforts received more and more attention, that 'milkshake moment' became the subject of countless discussions in the press and in classrooms, and many observers pointed out the lady's motive might have had less to do with the color of the kids' skin and more to do with the fact simply that they were kids.

It was a valid point -- an important one, even -- making it that much more significant that Greg had chosen to respond the way he did.

A Social Studies teacher observed, "History tells us that, more likely than not, the race of the students *was* a factor in that customer's decision to do what she did, but the valuable lesson comes from realizing that the way Greg chose to respond makes that whole debate moot. Had he said something to the lady about her being a racist and turned out to be wrong, that'd be one thing -- but he chose a response that focused on helping others instead of hurting her. As a result, we find ourselves able to focus on the benefits of what he did without fretting about what caused him to do it."

(14) People don't remember how you are treated.
They remember how you respond.

Greg felt good about what he did, but reality began to settle in a short time later. Before the return visit to Birchwood's Terrace could take place, he needed to find students who wanted to go, get their parents' permission *and* come up with a way to pay for the whole thing.

He began making calls all over the city. Within ten days, he'd rounded up seven kids and a parent to come with him back to Birchwood's -- but he still had no idea how he was going to pay for it.

With two days to go, as he headed over to The Club for another night on the job as a doorman, he decided he had just one option left -- talk to one of The Club's wealthy clients and ask them to foot the bill.

Greg knew the chance that a customer would grant that kind of request from a doorman was slim, and he knew he could lose his job just for asking -- but he decided it was a risk he had to take.

And it paid off.

The first customer Greg asked was the CEO of a local company. After hearing what the young doorman wanted to do and why he wanted to do it, The CEO not only agreed to pay for the brunch -- he said he'd join them.

So, that Sunday, Greg returned to Birchwood's Terrace just like he vowed he would. The ten people who came with him ended up being the seven kids and one parent, plus The CEO and one of The CEO's friends.

The brunch was everything Greg could have hoped for and more. The food and shakes were delicious, the staff treated them wonderfully, and everyone at the table had a great time.

And it was likely at that moment -- sipping a shake, surrounded by a diverse group of people all getting along -- that Greg knew he stumbled onto the world he always wanted to be part of -- a world where everybody could fit in, a world where people were co-existing *together* instead of merely co-existing *side by side*. And he knew he didn't want to see it end as quickly as it started. And so, he decided it wouldn't.

A week turned into a month and Greg was still returning every Sunday. Each week, he brought five to ten of his friends -- adults from every walk of life -- and an equal number of students -- kids from different races and backgrounds. The adults each paid for themselves and one kid. The students each paid a dollar to remind them "nothing in life is free."

In many ways, Greg was following the blueprint he mapped out in Louisiana -- giving kids a chance to meet people who could mentor them about college and careers -- but there was one big difference. This time, he was now also focusing on giving kids a chance to meet *each other* -- going out of his way to invite students from all different backgrounds to attend.

Some people questioned the value of including so-called *rich kids,* but Greg insisted on it. He said the only way to truly get kids from different backgrounds past the stereotypes they hear and read about each other was to bring them all together so they could actually meet face-to-face.

"And besides," he said, "kids whose parents have a lot of money need just as much guidance and help as any other kids do -- maybe even more."

In the process of bringing these multicultural groups together, Greg had created a full-fledged program. He even gave the group a name.

The Brunch Bunch.

It wasn't too fancy-sounding, but neither was the group. They were just a bunch of people going to brunch. Nothing more, nothing less.

Until, that is, Mr. Landers caught wind of them. Mr. Landers, whose company runs the MultiplexCLUBS, appreciated what Greg was trying to do and offered to let the group come play basketball after brunch since one of his health clubs happened to be just a few blocks from the restaurant.

After seeing how well the kids behaved, Mr. Landers said Greg could bring them back for an hour *every week.*

And just like that, The Brunch Bunch suddenly had a routine -- eat at Birchwood's every Sunday, then head over to the gym for an hour of fun.

As one kid said, "Milkshakes and b-ball, it doesn't get much better."

**

Birchwood's Terrace was not the only restaurant Greg visited every week. Every Tuesday, he always stopped by the same place to get lunch. He always ordered the same thing -- turkey and lettuce on a bagel (to go). One week, as he picked up his order, Greg told the Manager that he'd love to give bagels to the kids at school if she ever had any leftovers.

A week later, she gave him three bags full of them. The kids *loved* the bagels, and the Manager loved helping the community, so she began giving Greg more and more to pass out each week. Until, one time, she gave him more bagels than there were students in the whole school. He thought about just throwing away the extras, but then he decided against it. He knew somebody somewhere would want them. So, he walked around the neighborhood looking for a place to bring the bagels. In a matter of mere minutes, he found a spot to bring them -- a local center for seniors.

It was like his Grandma always said -- go that extra mile, and it usually only takes a couple steps to see something good come out of it.

The residents at The Center already had food so they didn't need the bagels, but they did seem to enjoy the company of an unexpected visitor -- and the feeling was clearly mutual. Despite his schedule, Greg began carving out enough time to visit The Center every Saturday afternoon.

Given the residents' physical condition, he felt an instinct to talk softly around them, but he soon discovered the error of his ways. Wheelchair-bound or not, the residents were young at heart. They wanted to argue about politics and hear jokes (and tell a few as well) and cheer on their favorite teams. More than anything, they loved to tell stories. They didn't just know history -- they had *lived* it -- and they loved to share it.

The more Greg got to know the residents, the more he liked them. They were respectful and worthy of respect, and above all else, they were kind. In one instance, after he mentioned his Grandma was under the weather, one of them gave him a bag with seven greeting cards so he could send her one every day of the week.

Before long, just as he did in Louisiana, Greg began asking his friends to come volunteer with him. Some were happy to do it. Others, frankly, were not too crazy about the idea of spending their free time with a "bunch of old people." But he stayed on their case until they went at least one time. And once they did, it usually didn't take long for them to realize why Greg liked it there so much. By the time the hour was up, most of his friends were already asking if and when they could come back.

(15) Assumptions and stereotypes work in all directions.
An elderly, white woman can be subjected to them
just as easily -- and unfairly -- as a young, black man.

In June, Greg's brief stint as a substitute teacher was scheduled to end.

For weeks, he carefully mapped out his final day. Instead of teaching, he decided to make a series of brief stops at all the schools he worked at throughout the year as a sub. He even convinced his mom to join him so she could see that his time as a sub had been time well spent.

It seemed a fitting end, but the day turned out to be a wreck -- capped off by an argument between Rose and an official at one of the schools.

To Greg, it was the same old story. After all his hard work, just as he was about to celebrate his success, something went terribly wrong.

He knew he should just put the day out of his mind and move on to the lucrative career in business that awaited him, but he just couldn't do it. He just couldn't stand the thought of ending things on such a bad note. And so, with the same prove-'em-wrong impulsiveness that caused him to transfer to Froehmann Whitfield instead of studying film in Europe as planned, he suddenly decided to take yet another detour.

"I'm going back to substitute teach in the fall," Greg declared.

"Are you serious?" Greg's girlfriend at the time, Sloane, asked.

"A thousand percent serious, Sloane. *One thousand percent.*"

He sounded certain, but deep down, he knew it would be easier said than done. Months earlier, he promised his parents that he'd interview for a corporate job after the year was up. There seemed to be no way out.

Until, that is, he came up with the loophole of all loopholes.

Technically speaking, he promised his parents he'd *interview* for a job. He never promised he would actually *get* one.

Over the next few weeks, he went on job interviews as promised -- but he purposely messed them up.

In one interview, he stood up and jumped an imaginary rope right there in the man's office. In another instance, Greg brought a bag full of bagels to the meeting -- *and started juggling them.* On a third occasion, when asked for a reference, he put down the name of a fourteen year old (The interviewer only discovered the 'executive' was actually fourteen years old when she called the boy's house and was told he would have to call her back because he was busy playing video games.)

In between purposely ruining interviews, Greg continued to help his students -- and continued to learn from them as well.

In one instance, Greg, Sloane, Charlie and Charlie's girlfriend took some kids to their first pro baseball game. One boy, Elliott, wanted to bring his glove so he could catch a foul ball, but Greg told him to forget it -- noting that he was a lot more likely to lose the glove than he was to catch a ball.

Elliott refused to give up -- and kept referring to it as "the" foul ball, as if it were already guaranteed that one was going to be hit in his direction. Not wanting to be late, Greg finally gave up and gave in to the boy's wish.

Sure enough, in the 7th inning, as 20,000 other fans watched on, Elliott leapt from his seat, reached his glove into the air and caught his foul ball.

(16) If you have an idea you believe in, hold your ground, be prepared and when the moment does arrive, reach up and grab it.

In the fall, having successfully ruined every interview he went on, Greg dusted off his substitute teacher badge and returned to the classroom.

His first day back was certainly a memorable one.

During third period, a drunk man ventured into the school parking lot, climbed on top of Greg's car and began to bash it with a brick. Greg dashed outside, but the damage was already done.

A guy sitting across the street encouraged Greg to keep the brick so nobody else would pick it up and wreck other cars with it.

Even though the man meant well, the comment seemed ridiculous. The Green was rapidly changing -- the infamous housing projects were being replaced by a community of upscale homes. As a result of the ongoing construction, there were hundreds of stray bricks throughout the area. Taking one brick off the street hardly seemed to do much good.

"What good is one brick?" Greg asked.

The man's response became another life lesson:

(17) One brick might not be much, but it's one brick better than none.

The situation was unfortunate, but it really was an exception. Despite all the supposed dangers lurking in The Green, Greg rarely had a problem in the neighborhood. In fact, most residents treated him with respect.

But that's not to say everyone everywhere appreciated his efforts.

From time to time, when he said he was a substitute teacher, at a dinner party for instance, there were people who asked if he was going to become a *real* teacher at some point.

They didn't mean any harm, but the question made Greg wince.

He knew subs weren't *full-time* teachers. And he'd be the first to admit he wasn't a *great* teacher. But being told he wasn't a *real* teacher was a definite sore spot for the guy who spent much of his life being told he didn't understand the difference between fiction and reality.

The school bell rang around three o'clock, but Greg's days usually lasted much longer. Most nights, he worked out at the gym and then spent an hour or two on the phone putting together that Sunday's brunch.

The program was taking up more time than he ever dreamed it would, but there was no turning back now. The Brunch Bunch had become a part of people's lives. Kids were becoming friends with other kids they would have otherwise never met. They were meeting all kinds of different adults and learning about all kinds of different careers -- a few of the kids even got offers to work part-time or during the holidays from the adults they impressed at brunch. And speaking of the adults, so many of them were now offering to volunteer that the program had a *waiting list.*

Make no mistake, The Brunch Bunch did not magically erase the barriers that have divided society for centuries. From time to time, there *were* moments of awkward silence -- and once in a while, there were people who felt downright uncomfortable sitting next to others from such different backgrounds. But the great majority of people who took part in the program got beyond those hang-ups, got to know the others at the table and realized their similarities far outweighed their differences.

Upon reaching the group's first anniversary, Greg began to bring them to other eateries around the city. From local delis to five star hotspots, the restaurant community really embraced the program. Some offered to waive the entire bill altogether. The Brunch Bunch Tour was off and running.

Greg's Saturday afternoons were spent volunteering, too -- at The Center. After a few months, Greg was even given an unofficial role -- Bingo caller. His role was simple -- sit at the head of the table and shout out the numbers for an hour -- but just like always, nothing in Greg's life went as simply as it should have.

One afternoon, he got banned from the game.

Greg's friends were astounded when they heard the news.

"How could you mess up calling Bingo numbers?" they asked.

Greg shrugged, "I like the residents so much that I just couldn't stand to see them lose. So, I started calling out numbers that ensured each of them got a chance to win and, I guess, eventually, someone caught on."

He meant well, and everyone at The Center knew it. So, they said they still wanted him to visit each week -- just no more calling Bingo numbers.

Greg's good intentions nearly cost him his job at The Club, too.

He enjoyed working there, but after several months, he was anxious to prove he could do more than just stand by a door and greet people.

So, as time went on, he started to take on more and more responsibility. Seating guests. Serving bread. Clearing dishes. Chatting with customers.

He thought he was doing a great job, and when The Boss asked to talk to him about all the tasks he was doing without being asked, he thought he was on the verge of getting a pat on the back and maybe even a raise.

As it turned out, he almost got fired.

"I know you mean well," The Boss said politely, "but you're so busy trying to help everyone else that you forget about doing your own job."

Greg replied, "That's true, but all I do is just stand there and hold a door and say 'hello' to people coming in and 'goodbye' to people going out. Aren't I doing a better job by running around and helping everyone?"

The Boss smiled and said, "Not when I pay you to stand in one place."

(18) A wheel is of no value to a car unless it is spinning in circles.

Greg quietly went back to doing the job he was hired to do -- stand by the door and greet the customers. Not that he really minded.

As the doorman at one of the most popular spots in town, he was in a unique position to meet all kinds of interesting people -- from his new girlfriend, Jordan, to some of the most powerful businessmen in the city.

He got to watch them, to observe them, to try and figure out what made them so successful. In the process, he also learned what not to do.

More than once, for example, he saw wealthy customers talking to a busboy or parking attendant like they were parents scolding a small child.

Even when the customers meant well, some gave into stereotypes. One time, for example, a lady urged Greg to keep working hard and saving his money until he could afford to go to college (assuming -- incorrectly -- that he must not have a college degree if he was working as a doorman).

(19) The only thing you should assume about a person
based on their job...is that they have one

In June, Greg's *second* year as a substitute came to an end, and he went on another series of job interviews -- and this time, he actually wanted to get hired. He still planned to volunteer on the weekends, but Charlie and the others from back home were now well on their way climbing the corporate ladder, and Greg was anxious to catch up.

It turned out there was just one small problem with his plan.

Nobody wanted to hire him.

Most interviewers said a "substitute teaching restaurant doorman" was not exactly what they were looking for. Others felt he was too concerned with helping people to focus on anything else -- let alone a full-time job. In the end, for one reason or another, not one single company offered him a full-time position of any kind.

With his own personal dreams slipping away, Greg did what he always did -- distracted himself from thinking about it by helping other people.

He continued volunteering at The Center every Saturday. The brunch program kept meeting on Sundays -- 70 straight weeks and counting. He even arranged for a company to donate the money and time needed to build an entire garden inside the empty atrium of a grade school in The Green.

Greg was proud of his efforts, but as long as he was focusing on helping others, he just wished he could do it on a grander scale. And that's when Harvard Charlie told him there was a way that he could. All he had to do was set up something called a Not-For-Profit company.

As it was explained to Greg, a *For-Profit* company is one which sells products or services in an effort to make money, like a company that sells shoes or computers. A *Not-For-Profit* company, on the other hand, is focused on providing a service to society like helping those in need.

And, Harvard Charlie explained, a lot of people and companies who like to donate money will *only* donate money to groups that are officially recognized as Not-For-Profit companies.

Greg had no experience running a Not-For-Profit company and had no real idea what was involved, but he wanted to get as much help as possible for the students, so he agreed to do it anyway.

"And besides," he said, "if the goal is to *not* make a profit, I mean, to *not* make money? How hard could that be?"

People assumed the new group would be called The Brunch Bunch Foundation, but Greg quickly rejected that idea. He said his organization was going to do much more than just take kids to brunch. One day, he said, they would send kids to college -- and he wanted a name which reflected that broader vision.

The name he ended up choosing was *The 11-10-02 Foundation.*

11-10-02 stood for Greg's 30th birthday, November 10, 2002, and his belief people under thirty were as capable as anyone when it came to making a difference.

The unusual name caused a lot of people to scratch their heads -- "11-10-02 sounds like the combination to my locker," one kid joked -- but even more than the odd name, it was Greg's inexperience that people questioned. Nobody seemed to believe a 25 year old substitute teaching restaurant doorman could run something of this nature.

Nobody, that is, except his Grandma.

She told him all he had to do was the same thing he'd done all his life -- just keep failing until you succeed -- and eventually the Foundation would prosper. She said the only real question was if he would be willing to set aside his own goals like law school and writing long enough to do it.

He looked her in the eye and said he was willing to spend as much time as it took to build a foundation that could change the world.

His Grandma smiled and said, "In that case, there's just one more thing you need. A place to sit."

"How come?" Greg asked.

"Because this is going to take so long that if you don't have a place to sit, your feet are going to hurt."

And with that, she gave him her rocking chair.

The gift from his Grandma reminded Greg of the lesson he learned as a child reading books -- as long as you have time, the willingness to spend it and the place to sit, you can make a difference.

His spirits were lifted even further when the Foundation received its first donation -- $100 from a couple named the Gutheim's -- but it didn't take long before that excitement wore off and Greg realized his Grandma wasn't kidding. Between the papers to fill out and the decisions to make, the Foundation took up more time than he could have ever imagined -- and using his free time to get it all done wasn't an option because there simply wasn't any free time left.

The first step he took was a costly one -- quitting his part-time job as a doorman. He learned a lot from The Boss, liked his co-workers, and enjoyed the customers, but he just didn't have a choice. He needed *time*.

The extra hours did help, but he still needed more time *during* the week when he could call people at work. He decided to use his lunch break to do it. He knew ten minutes a day wasn't much, but he figured it was ten minutes more than nothing. So, he searched around Blue Academy for a place to sit and make calls.

Until, finally, he found a room on the 4th floor. It wasn't very big -- the size of a walk-in closet -- and half of it was taken up by a dishwashing bin -- but it had a phone and a desk, so Greg took it. He declared it to be his "first office" and even hung up a "Boardroom" sign on the ledge.

It turned out there was just one small problem.

It was The Lunch Lady's desk and phone, that dishwashing bin was where she and her two co-workers cleaned the trays, and nobody else was supposed to enter that room without her permission -- let alone start putting things up on the ledge.

Everyone figured she would kick Greg out, but she never did -- letting him use her desk for five to ten minutes each day.

On the surface, the two seemed to be a very odd couple -- different genders, ages, races, religions, cultures and backgrounds -- but they enjoyed each other's company. The Lunch Lady was amused by Greg's grand dreams and admired his desire to help others. In turn, he admired her work ethic, and her no-nonsense approach reminded him of his Grandma.

The extra ten minutes a day did help Greg get more done, and an article in the local paper about what he was doing helped bring in a few donations -- but the guy hoping to change the world was still raising little more than spare change. When even the most basic supplies seemed too expensive, Greg turned to his new friend, The Lunch Lady, for guidance.

"Just do the best you can with what you have," she said.

The advice added up to all of ten words, but after she said it, he started treating everything in his apartment like it was *sacred*. A lunchbox was now a briefcase. Empty cereal boxes became filing cabinets. That brick he kept after the man beat up his car with it? It was now a paper weight. Jordan sighed, "Even his refrigerator was used to store files."

(20) Make what you have be what you need

With a makeshift office of his own starting to take shape, Greg focused on how to spread the word about his new group. He decided the internet was the perfect way to start. Night after night, he sat at his computer and taught himself how to make a website.

The one he put together was not too fancy, but it was effective -- and more donations started trickling in. One of them was a check for *five thousand dollars* from a couple named the Millner's. When Greg saw it, he started running around in circles, waving the check in the air and hollering. It was the single biggest check he'd ever held in his life.

Knowing there were people who believed so strongly in what he was doing, Greg felt motivated to look for ways to raise even more money. Harvard Charlie suggested he write letters to companies who donate lots of money to charity every year and ask them for support.

Greg gave it his best shot -- spending hours and hours filling out forms and writing proposals -- but every response was the same. *No.*

As the rejections started piling up, he felt like a high school senior all over again. He wanted to tear up the letters into little pieces, but his Grandma insisted he should do the exact opposite.

"We've been through this," she huffed. "Rejection is something to be *proud* of. You don't throw out letters like that. You *frame* them."

Accepting rejection letters was one thing -- turning them into art seemed like quite another -- but Greg did as she suggested. He literally framed a stack of the rejection letters and hung them on his wall.

It would not be the only time Greg's Grandma gave him advice that left him scratching his head.

When he continued to struggle in his efforts to raise the millions of dollars he hoped to raise, she told him, "Instead of trying to change the whole world, just start with the world outside your window."

Greg was crushed. The way he figured, you don't tell someone to focus on small dreams unless you think they can't reach big ones.

A few days later, when he attended that Sunday's brunch, her words were still weighing on his mind. As he sulked in silence, the other people at the table realized something was wrong.

After he explained why he was upset, one of the kids, Trace, tried to cheer him up by pointing out that even superheroes like Batman focus their efforts on just one city, not the entire world.

Another kid, Josh, offered words of encouragement, too.

"Your Grandma didn't say *stay* small. She just said *start* small. You know, like you start small, then one day, you get big."

The more Greg thought about what Trace and Josh said, the more his Grandma's advice started making sense. Instead of waiting until he raised enough money to fund the college scholarships he dreamed of, he decided he would use what he'd raised so far to make a smaller but immediate difference to help his local community.

(21) Before you try and change the world,
focus on the world outside your window.

Looking out his apartment window, Greg could see hundreds of locations throughout The Green that might benefit from his group's help, but it took less than a minute for him to pinpoint where he wanted to start.

Blue Academy.

The school had a special place outside his window -- exactly four blocks to the west -- and a special place in his heart. It was where he spent his first day as a sub, where those first two kids he took for shakes went to school, and where he shared an "office" with the Lunch Lady.

Admittedly, Blue didn't look like much on the outside -- the bright paint had started to chip off long ago, and the windows seemed dark and worn down -- but Greg had gotten far beyond that first impression.

He was especially struck by Principal Brooks and his staff. Sometimes, they didn't have enough books or supplies, but like The Lunch Lady said, they just did the best they could with what they had. Even on the long days, the teachers went out of their way to support each other.

To Greg, they were exactly what educators should be -- and everything he was trying so hard to be.

There was no doubt in his mind. Blue Academy was the school he wanted to help first. And sooner than he expected, he had a chance to do it.

One day, he asked the kind-hearted clerk, Ms. Boggs, if he could have a school t-shirt to wear around town. She smiled warmly and said she appreciated his school pride -- but there was no way she could give him one. Blue Academy had no school shirts -- they couldn't afford them.

Greg couldn't believe his ears. How can kids be expected to take pride in their school if they can't wear shirts with its name across the front? He knew right away this was a perfect chance for his young foundation to help make a small but lasting difference. He went home, designed new shirts for the school, then promptly ordered six hundred.

A few weeks later, Principal Brooks arranged a special assembly for Greg to unveil the shirts. The school didn't have a gym or auditorium, so the event had to take place in the dimly lit first floor hallway. And the hall was small, so only half the school got to attend. It was a lot different than what Greg always dreamed his first "big" speech would be like, but he didn't seem to mind one bit. In fact, as he watched the kids' faces light up after discovering what was inside the boxes, he never seemed happier.

His Grandma, Trace and Josh were right.

Making a small difference is still a big thing.

In the days that followed, the Foundation started giving grants to other schools -- helping kids and teachers with books, supplies and computers.

Each grant the Foundation gave out was named after one of Greg's favorite old instructors -- from his 1st grade teacher to his professors from college. He appreciated them when he was a student, but he appreciated them even more now that he realized how hard it is to be a good teacher.

The kids seemed grateful for the help from Greg and his foundation, but truth be told, more times than he could count, he felt like it was *the students* helping and teaching *him* and not the other way around.

When Greg was upset someone had not treated him nicely, it was a kid who put his feelings back in perspective with a note about a time when someone was "*really* not treated nicely" -- when her cousin was killed. (Greg was so struck by the note he ended up keeping it in his wallet).

When Good Morning America announced they would be burying a Time Capsule that featured Greg's civic efforts and he showed up at school that day feeling a little too self-important, it was a kid who pointed out he was wearing two different shoes and instantly put him right back in his place. (Greg's Grandma loved the story so much that she ordered Greg to start wearing mismatched socks every day -- so that a single glance at his feet would remind him how quickly and easily the child humbled him.)

And those were just two examples of many.

Time and time again, Greg left school at the end of the day with a new lesson he learned from the kids he was supposedly teaching and helping.

**

After the speech at Blue Academy, Greg began getting invited to speak at other schools about overcoming obstacles and helping others. Each time, he opted to speak from the heart instead of writing a speech or using notes.

His friends often joked that, given how much he rambled, he was asking for disaster -- but in front of a microphone, he was like a whole different person. He spoke slowly and clearly, and he never went longer than the time allotted to him. A teacher who attended a speech later wrote that Greg's words were "calm and surreal, and floated through the air."

Of all the invitations Greg received, none were sweeter than when he was invited back to his old high school to speak at an all-school assembly.

It was the triumphant return he had been imagining for years.

When Greg arrived at Mortimer Dowhill, all his old teachers who were still working there came up to greet him.

All his old teachers, that is, except one.

Avery P. Welton.

When Mr. Welton entered the room, he took a seat without saying a single word. To add insult to injury, he wouldn't even look at the podium.

In an instant, Greg could feel his blood pressure starting to rise and that old anger bubbling back toward the surface. Part of him was tempted to start shouting at Welton until they turned off the microphone.

But he resisted the urge to do it.

Looking out at the smiling faces of all his other old teachers who had always been kind to him, looking out at the impressionable teenagers sitting beside them, he just couldn't do it. The school had asked him -- and trusted him -- to send a positive message to those students, and no matter how upset he was, that's what he was going to do.

So instead of bringing up Mr. Welton and The Letter, he spoke instead about all the *good* things he remembered about the school and the teachers there who had such a positive influence on his life. And then, he talked to the kids about diversity and service -- using his brunch program and his foundation as examples for them to think about.

In his heart, Greg hoped that taking the higher road would lead to something positive -- perhaps, Welton would finally apologize after all these years. But after the speech, the man still did not say a word to him.

Not to admit he was wrong all those years ago. Not to congratulate Greg on his success in college. Not to commend him for making a difference in the community. Not to thank him for avoiding mention of the letter of "recommendation" during the speech. Not even to say hello.

Not one single word.

Greg headed back home feeling sick about the experience.

What happened to a positive attitude leading to positive results?

And then, just when he was *this close* to being convinced that his effort to stay positive had been pointless, he found out about Clifford.

A sophomore at MDCR, Clifford had reached an inspiring conclusion after hearing Greg's speech. He too wanted to make a difference, and he too wanted to do it now instead of later. In the days that followed, without telling anyone, Cliff started writing letters to companies all over the country asking them to help Greg send kids to college.

The boy's efforts did not succeed, but the mere fact that he tried was more than enough to brighten Greg's spirits when he found out. Something positive *had* come out of him staying positive after all. And as fate would have it, Cliff's *something positive* inspired another student to do the same.

When a high school junior named Fitz heard about what Cliff did to try and help others, Fitz decided he could do something, too.

Fitz decided to assemble a jazz group and throw a concert with all the proceeds going to The 11-10-02 Foundation. Over the next few months, Fitz and his pals practiced songs, passed out fliers and told everyone they knew about the show. They even got their principal to let them use the school auditorium.

As Greg sat in the audience listening to the concert, he nearly burst with pride. Going back to his days in Louisiana, his goal had always been to inspire others to help him bring people together. So, the efforts of Fitz and his jazz band were -- literally -- music to his ears.

The Foundation was beginning to blossom, but that is not to say Greg's own path was getting any easier. He continued to face one roadblock after another. In the fall, that obstacle became his feet.

Seemingly out of nowhere, Greg found himself unable to walk without pain. According to the doctor, the problem required surgery.

At first, Greg viewed the news that he would need to spend a few days off his feet as a vacation -- expecting a wheelchair to be like the Big Wheel he rode when he was a boy. Against doctor's orders, he even insisted on -- literally -- wheeling himself home from the hospital after the surgery.

He was quite the sight to behold -- laughing and singing as he inched his bandaged body down the street.

Once he finally made it home and the medicine wore off, he quickly got a rude awakening. Three days in a wheelchair proved to be one of the most humbling experiences of his life. In the process, he developed a newfound respect for the strength possessed by people who deal with physical obstacles every day of their life.

The operation didn't stop Greg's streak of brunches -- the had the kids wheel him to the table -- but it was a close call. And it wasn't the only one.

Greg overcame every obstacle imaginable to keep The Streak alive. There were blizzards, heat waves and the day his car broke down ten minutes before a brunch. Not to mention, birthday parties, weddings, anniversaries, and sometimes, he was sick or just plain tired.

But in the end, nothing ever got in the way of his Streak.

Two months later, Greg had the same operation on the other foot -- and was back in a wheelchair for three more days. Within a week, he was back on his feet, but he no longer could run around as freely as he once did.

His Grandma insisted it was a blessing in disguise.

She said, "If you have to walk slower, it takes you longer to get somewhere, and the longer it takes you to get somewhere, the more you appreciate getting there once you finally do. And besides, if it makes you stay off your feet, then you get more time to work on things like your art."

As always, she was right.

He spent more time on his sketches, and sure enough, the better they seemed to get. In fact, the kid who could barely draw a straight line had slowly but surely begun drawing portraits that were practically *lifelike*.

The drawings had gotten *so* good that, one afternoon, a repairman broke into Greg's apartment just to see the originals framed on the walls.

"I wasn't going to take anything," the man insisted, when questioned later. "I just wanted to see if he'd drawn anything new since I was there to fix his sink."

Most of the time, Greg drew leaders throughout history and his favorite characters from film. And so, his portrait of a real president was framed right alongside his portrait of an actor who portrayed a president in a movie. Just like everything else with Greg, his wall of framed drawings became a distinctly odd blend of fiction and reality.

And the more time Greg spent on his art, the more those lines seemed to blur. As he drew the pictures, he got carried away into the worlds of the people he was drawing -- imagining their friends, their families, their fate.

One of Greg's most prized portraits was his drawing of Martin Luther King, Jr. He hung it on his wall right by his desk. And so, in an ironic way, seven years after Greg left Louisiana, he still felt like Dr. King was looking over his shoulder.

As it turned out, art did more than just flex the muscles of Greg's imagination. It also helped him become a little more patient. He spent weeks on each drawing -- perfecting every hair, wrinkle and freckle --- before framing them and putting them up on his wall.

For a guy who rarely wanted to sit still let alone sit still *and silent*, art seemed to be just what the doctor ordered.

More than anything, art helped him develop *perspective*. He learned that when he was drawing a mouth, for example, he had to think about two things at once. Besides focusing on how the mouth looked, he also had to consider how that piece fit into the larger puzzle -- the face -- he was putting together. Over time, he realized the lesson applied to more than art. In life, there are always those two processes at work -- what you are doing at the moment and how that moment factors into the bigger picture.

> *(22) A well-drawn mouth can still turn a portrait into a cartoon*
> *if it is drawn next to a nose instead of beneath it.*

In between drawing portraits, Greg worked on the Foundation's logo. He had been trying to come up with one ever since the group began. A year and a half later, he finally came up with the symbol he wanted.

TM

Greg insisted it was *perfect*, but others were not so sure. In fact, most of his friends openly laughed when they saw what he drew.

"It looks like something a fifth grader would do!" one friend howled.

They were only teasing him, but in a sense, they were right. The logo *was* drawn by a 5th grader. Because, after all these years, Greg finally drew a picture that represented the things he saw outside his childhood window. From top to bottom, the images in the logo represented The Silhouette Man, The Ladder Horse, the three bushes and his puppy's grave (beneath the middle bush). The triangle that connected all the dots? It represented the tent Greg used to put up in the yard on the weekends.

Harvard Charlie could not believe his eyes when he saw it.

"Are you crazy? You weren't supposed to draw a picture of what you saw out your window when you were a little boy. You were supposed to come up with a serious image that represents the Foundation."

Charlie was just trying to help, but his words upset Greg greatly.

As kids, the two lived parallel lives -- the same schools, same camps and (it was expected) same bright future -- but somewhere along the way, their lives drifted in distinctly different directions. Charlie followed the path that was "expected" -- the Ivy Leagues, then corporate America, and now, a top business school. Greg, on the other hand, jumped off the "fast track" and carved out a much less certain one that included stops in Louisiana, The Club and The Green. Charlie wore $800 suits, carried a briefcase, traveled the world and took his dates out to elegant restaurants. Greg wore mismatched socks, carried a lunchbox, rarely ventured beyond the world outside his window and took his dates to local diners with coupons he'd clipped out of the paper.

Greg didn't mind that their paths veered in such different directions. He was genuinely happy for his pal's success. It was just that Greg's dad, Mark, reminded him on a daily basis that Charlie was living the life he "could be and should be" living. So instead of taking the comment for what it was -- advice from a friend -- Greg saw it as the guy he was "supposed to be" telling him what he was "supposed to do" -- and he couldn't stand it.

"Just because Charlie has a fancy business school on his resume," Greg griped, "it doesn't mean he's always right and I'm always wrong."

Greg's Grandma told him to quit his complaining.

"Stop comparing yourself to Charlie," she huffed. "I don't care what your father says. Charlie is Charlie. Greg is Greg. The only person you oughtta compare yourself to is the guy in the mirror. If you're doing better than you were doing a year ago, then you're doing just fine. That's the only competition that matters."

(23) The only person you should ever compare yourself to is...yourself.

As always, the advice helped -- but ironically enough, in this instance, Greg really shouldn't have worried about what Charlie said.

The fact of the matter was his logo was a lot more complex than Charlie or anyone else realized. Yes, its different parts were inspired by what Greg saw outside his childhood window, but that was just Phase One. Every part of the logo had a *second* meaning.

The Three Ovals were not just three bushes. They also represented three glasses -- symbolizing the day Greg and two kids had milkshakes -- the three shakes that eventually led to the start of The Brunch Bunch.

The Tombstone represented the tombstone in Greg's old yard. It also represented the philosophy that he first learned from his brief friendship with the puppy who was buried there -- seize the chance to get to know people today because there's no guarantee they'll still be there tomorrow.

The Ladder represented The Ladder Horse in the backyard. It also represented what the kids were being taught at brunch -- the ladder's five rungs symbolizing five principles that lead to a successful future: ethics, etiquette, effort, education and environment.

The Silhouette on top of the ladder represented The Silhouette Man swing set in Greg's old backyard. It also represented the idea that if a kid took the lessons taught at brunch to heart, then he or she will have climbed the ladder's five rungs and made themselves, and the program, a success.

The Triangle represented the tent Greg used to put up in the backyard. It also represented a mountain, and the belief that it was good to make a big deal out of something small -- to make a mountain out of a molehill -- if it's done for the right reason. And that's what Greg had done with The Brunch Bunch -- turning a couple shakes into a full-fledged program.

As Greg's feet healed, he continued trying to help others whenever he could -- whether it was hosting the weekly brunches now on the verge of their three year anniversary, bringing more friends with him to volunteer at The Center, surprising a hard-working music teacher with a grant for more instruments, or dressing up as Santa Claus on Christmas Eve and delivering gifts to a church in The Green.

He hoped his efforts would inspire other people to do something, too. And that's exactly what happened.

In some cases, people were inspired to support his goals -- signing up for a brunch, volunteering to come with him to The Center, or making donations to The 11-10-02 Foundation. Sometimes, they were Greg's friends -- one of his old camp counselors sent him a brand new desk -- but other times, they were complete strangers -- a woman in Oklahoma sent a brand new fax machine.

In other cases, people heard about Greg's efforts and were inspired to set new goals of their own. More than once, he got a note from someone who said his story inspired them to go back to school to be a teacher.

As the weeks passed, the story continued to spread. Every other month, it seemed like something unusual was happening.

At the start of the new year, an English teacher assigned Greg's story as part of a unit on tolerance and diversity, along with *Schindler's List* by Steven Spielberg and *Night* by Elie Wiesel. Two months later, President Clinton sent The Brunch Bunch Kids a letter encouraging them to continue their efforts to celebrate diversity. Two months after that, Greg and his Grandma graced the cover of *Senior News*. And then, there was a New York fashion magazine that did an article *about what Greg wore* -- even running a picture of his mismatched socks.

Despite the unusual twists and turns, Greg was determined to stay focused. With that in mind, he returned to his hometown to speak at his old middle school and announce a special grant in honor of one of the teachers who tried especially hard to help him when he was a boy. And then, he traveled to Bailey's hometown to speak at *his* old school and announce a grant from the Foundation that would help the students there.

The grant wasn't the only honor Greg named after the friend he met at football camp nearly a decade earlier. He decided to name The 11-10-02 Foundation's first college scholarship in Bailey's memory, too.

And with the money in place to fund it thanks to another $5,000 gift, all Greg had to do now was decide which student got it. To help narrow the field, he contacted eleven schools and told them they could each nominate two seniors. In turn, the nominees were all asked to prepare an application.

To pick the winner, Greg asked a dozen of his friends to review the applications. They agreed to do it, but they quickly realized judging was no easy task. It was so hard, in fact, that they could not choose between two of the finalists.

Fortunately, before Greg had to think of a way to break the deadlock, somebody solved the problem for him. One judge was so impressed by the nominees that he started making calls and raised the money for a second scholarship so both kids could win.

The Foundation not only had its first ever Scholar. It now had *two*.

This was something Greg pictured for years, and it definitely called for a celebration. He chose a place called Maggiano's Little Italy to be the site of the party. The Brunch Bunch had eaten there a number of times over the past couple years. The food was always amazing, and they were always treated like kings. Given that Maggiano's also had a separate banquet room that could cater to several hundred people, it seemed to be a perfect fit.

After Greg booked the space, Maggiano's Banquets Manager called him to plan the menu, but to her surprise, he asked her to do it on her own.

It seemed out of character for a guy who focused on every detail to ask someone else to make the decisions, but truth be told, he wasn't concerned about what the audience ate. He was worried about what they *saw*.

Twenty years after setting foot in the movie theater for the first time, seven years after he passed up the chance to study film in Europe, and four years after his brief trip to California, Greg still yearned for the chance to tell stories that changed people's lives -- and this was going to be his chance to do that. This was going to be his *show*.

And he wasted little time getting started with its production.

The first decision was easy -- the musical entertainment. Without a second thought, Greg invited Fitz and his pals to be the band -- out of appreciation for the concert they put together a few months earlier.

With that out of the way, Greg began to focus on the trophies.

Some of his friends couldn't understand why it really mattered -- trophies are trophies, they said, the scholarship winners will just be happy to get one -- but Greg insisted it was an important decision.

He said, "Every great story has a *symbol*. Willy Wonka, he had those golden tickets. Forrest Gump, he had shrimp. I gotta have one, too."

He spent hours pouring through catalogs looking for a design that was unique, but none of them fit what he was looking for. Until finally, he decided to just design his own...*using unwashed milkshake glasses*.

Greg's friends thought he was nuts, but he insisted it was perfect.

"For one thing," he told them, "they symbolize the day I took the kids for shakes that led to all this. But more importantly, the whole point is we're trying to show that everything and everyone has value -- and what better way is there to prove that than by turning moldy, dirty milkshake glasses into trophies?!"

After getting Mr. Goldberg the Trophy Maker to agree to make the trophies (despite the horrible smell), Greg turned his attention to selling tickets. Since there was no budget for invitations, he just started walking around the neighborhood and talking to everyone he passed.

Not too many were impressed by the 'gala' he was promoting.

After hearing Greg's sales pitch on the street, one observer said, "It seemed like a cute little event, but it certainly wasn't a *gala*. A gala is a fancy affair on a Saturday night at a big hotel. This was going to take place *on a Sunday...at a restaurant* -- with no sponsors, no invitations, and the band was a bunch of kids. I'm sorry, but that's no gala."

Not surprisingly, a whopping total of six tickets were purchased the first week -- but ticket sales were hardly Greg's only source of frustration. As spring became summer, he became more and more frustrated with the media.

On the one hand, when they wrote about The Foundation or talked about it on TV, they always said nice things -- and the positive attention did help the young organization attract new supporters. On the other hand, some of the reporters used labels like *underprivileged* and *disadvantaged* to describe the people Greg helped, and it frustrated him to no end.

Having listened to his students talk about the issue, there was no doubt in his mind that the labels were hurtful -- *"How would you like it if the media ran a story about you, and then, for no reason, the reporter belittles how and where you were raised?"* -- and he was equally certain the labels were the result of a double standard -- *"When's the last time you saw a headline like 'Overprivileged kid wins spelling bee'?"* -- and unfair -- *"Why does the media get to decide what a privilege is?"* -- and misleading -- *"Less fortunate than who?"* -- as well as hypocritical -- *"Why write an article praising someone's efforts to break stereotypes if you're just gonna use those stereotypes in the story?"* -- so why would anyone use them???

He griped about it on a daily basis until, finally, his Grandma spoke up.

"You're giving me a headache," she huffed. "If you've got something to say, just do what they do -- write it down -- and try not to ramble."

He did as she told him -- writing down his feelings about stereotypes and labels. When he was done, he submitted his one page essay to the paper as a guest column (and kept submitting it until they finally agreed to run it).

He knew his column in and of itself certainly wouldn't solve the problem, but it was, at least, *something*.

Of all the lines he wrote, his favorite was the one which he'd been repeating to the students over and over again for three years and which his Grandma had been repeating to him all his life.

The most important word in the world is your name.

And it was with that line in mind that the guest column ended with something that had not seen the light of day very often since Greg was a boy. His *full* name -- middle name, Forbes, included.

Having spent so much time telling kids to take pride in their name, he decided it was time to finally embrace his own.

**

Greg had evolved from a shy little child into a young man bursting with confidence. Even socially, he was finally coming into his own. The boy who used to stutter when he saw the pretty girl with blue eyes was now being featured in magazines as one of the most eligible men in the city.

"Hot! Hot! Hot!" declared one headline.

Greg thought the articles were a bit silly, but given the teasing he took as a kid, it did not take long for the affection to go to his head.

And just like always, it took even less time for him to be humbled right back to reality.

When being primped and prepped for one of the magazine photo shoots, Mister Eligible suddenly noticed some black dust in the air.

"What's that?" he asked the hair stylist.

"Just powder," she replied. "to cover up the shine from your head."

He didn't understand what she meant, so she picked up a mirror and showed him. When he saw what she was pointing at, his heart sank to his stomach. A clump of his hair was missing.

Charlie said, "It wasn't the end of the world, but you still had to feel bad for the guy. He was such a scrawny kid for so long, and here he was, after all those years in the gym, just when he felt like he had a reason to be proud of the way he looked, his hair suddenly starts falling out. It's like, if it wasn't one thing, it was always another."

As he'd done so many times before, Greg tried to just block the whole thing out by focusing on helping other people address their problems.

In the meantime, word of his community efforts just kept on spreading.

In the spring, he was chosen by the local NBC station for one of the nation's most prized civic honors -- the Jefferson Award for Public Service.

As summer arrived, Greg boarded a plane for the National Jefferson Awards (after missing the first flight, of course). A product of the AIPS, the National Jefferson Awards are an annual event in Washington D.C. that recognizes people making a difference on the "local" and "national" level.

The trip turned out to be one of the most incredible experiences of Greg's life. In the span of just three days, he attended a reception with U.S. Senators, a dinner with the likes of former astronaut John Glenn and a ceremony in the Supreme Court with Justice Sandra Day O'Connor. He also met the President of the United States and even walked the President's dog around the West Wing of the White House.

And, not surprisingly, despite being there for just one half of one week, Greg also managed to have a few of his typical adventures. In one instance, he took a wrong turn while looking for the bathroom and interrupted a reporter doing a broadcast for the nightly news. In another case, he strolled into the train station, unaware that a major motion picture was in the process of being filmed there. Most memorable of all, he misread his schedule and showed up to a suit-and-tie breakfast *in his pajamas.*

"I thought it meant for me to go to breakfast, *then* put on a suit and tie," he explained to the shocked organizers. (Not that he really seemed too concerned. While a hundred guests in suits and dresses watched on in amazement, Greg went ahead and sat down in his pajamas and ate two plates full of pancakes before going back to his room to change).

From beginning to end, the three days in D.C. were unforgettable. In the end, though, it was the forty other local Jefferson Award winners who were there -- 36 adults and four kids -- whose stories touched Greg most.

They were living proof of what Greg believed ever since he was a child reading about Harriet Tubman -- that anyone anywhere at any age can make a difference. It was fun to rub elbows with Senators, the President and a Supreme Court Justice, but the other local award winners -- *they* were the ones who Greg felt defined what public service was really all about. Ordinary, every day people making an extraordinary difference.

Greg was most inspired by one of the four student honorees -- an eleven year old boy from Kentucky named Jarrett. The fact he was even alive was a miracle -- having spent his life battling cancer, already losing his hair and one leg in the process. And yet, instead of dwelling on his own problems, the boy started an organization to brighten up the lives of other kids facing similar obstacles.

Greg marveled at the boy's positive attitude. Jarrett had so much *inner* strength that he continued to have the confidence of a heavyweight champ, even as his physical condition grew worse. It was a humbling reminder that there's a lot more to life than how much weight you can lift and whether there's a shiny reflection off the top of your head.

(24) Don't judge a person by what you can see.
Don't judge a person by what you cannot see, either.

Less than two weeks later, it was the last Sunday in June, and the Gala at Maggiano's was just a few short hours away. Despite having no sponsors or invitations, the event had somehow sold out.

With a 'full house' expected for the big show, Greg wanted to check and double-check all the details, but it was a luxury he just didn't have. Gala or no gala, Sunday afternoon still meant it was time for brunch.

And this one was going to be special.

Greg's 172nd brunch in a row was going to be the very last one.

He had promised his parents he'd go to law school or get a corporate

job once he fulfilled his goal of sending a kid to college. And if he chose
something out of state, the streak of brunches was bound to end.

Rather than drag it out, he decided to just bring everything to an end on
one, grand unforgettable day. And this was going to be that day.

For the final outing, Greg thought about a reunion of the hundreds of
people who'd come to at least one brunch over the years. But as the day
grew closer, he had a change of heart -- deciding it would be more fitting to
end the streak of brunches the exact same way it started.

One man, two kids and three milkshakes.

So just past noon, without any fanfare, Greg and two kids -- Trace and
Josh -- made the short walk to go get a bite to eat, gulp down some shakes
and bring the streak of brunches to a simple and quiet end.

At least, that was the plan.

When they arrived, the restaurant refused to let Greg in.

Not that he should've been surprised. After all, he had not chosen just
any restaurant. This was Dorothy Keyser's Place.

Two years earlier, when Greg first started bringing The Brunch Bunch
to different restaurants around the city, there was only one spot in town
that did not agree to give the group a discount -- Keyser's Place.

Rather than accept the possibility that they could not afford to do it, or
that they already supported their fill of worthy causes, or that they simply
didn't like to support any causes, Greg took it *personally* -- convinced that
the head of the restaurant was trying to undermine the program's success.

It was the same insecurity Greg displayed over and over again ever
since Mr. Welton betrayed him nearly a decade earlier. If someone --
especially someone in a position of authority -- didn't fully support his
plan, he became convinced that they were actively trying to undermine it.

And when he felt that way, he almost always lashed out with long,
rambling notes oozing with self-righteous anger.

Rose said, "It was painful to watch because you knew the letters
weren't going to accomplish a thing, other than upsetting the people who
received them, but you also knew that there was no way you could get him
to stop writing them. After what happened with Welton, if he saw someone
interfering with his dreams -- or anyone's dreams for that matter -- he felt
like it was his personal responsibility to say something."

His friends warned him that there would eventually be a price to pay.

Greg's business-wise friend, Abby, said, "I know this is an important
thing to you to write these letters, but people have long memories, Greg,
and sooner or later, you're going to want something from one of these
people, and they're going to say no because they're still upset about some
dumb letter you wrote a few years earlier."

And, sure enough, that's exactly what happened with Keyser's Place.

After they didn't support the brunches, Greg wrote a note complaining about Keyser's management. Two years later, they had not forgotten the sting of his words. So much so, they not only wouldn't give him a discount -- now, apparently, they wouldn't even serve him.

Not knowing the history between Greg and the restaurant, Josh and Trace were stunned by how he was treated, but they were even more surprised by his response. The same man who protested even the smallest injustice walked away from this one with a whimper -- taking the boys to another restaurant a few doors down and acting like nothing happened.

Trace said, "I didn't really know what to make of it. I thought maybe, with this being the last brunch in such a long streak, he just wanted to end things on a positive note -- so when they wouldn't let him in, he dropped it as quickly as possible so it didn't ruin things. At least, that was my best guess because once we got to the other restaurant, he never discussed it."

Three hours later

The sold-out Gala at Maggiano's was scheduled to start at exactly twenty-five minutes after six.

Despite looking forward to the night for months, when six-fifteen rolled around, Greg was nowhere to be found. Sitting out in the sun, he had -- as always -- gotten distracted and lost track of time.

When the host did finally show up just minutes before dinner was to be served, he announced that he "forgot" the seating chart -- so people could sit at any table they wanted. In truth, Greg never made one -- hoping the Gala could be just like the brunches where people walked in as strangers and walked away with new friends.

The guests all sported suits and dresses -- except for a kid named Rockefeller ('Rocky' to his friends), who was decked out in a tuxedo.

"If it's a Gala to you," the boy said to Greg, "then it's a Gala to me."

Greg smiled warmly at the remark. From the very first time they met, Rocky had been one of his favorite students -- hard-working in school (and even more so out of school, working full-time to help pay the bills), always polite to his classmates and teachers, plus he had the fancy-sounding kind of name that Greg Forbes could appreciate.

Once Rockefeller and the other guests chose their seats, they ate to their hearts' content as the sound of jazz filled the air.

When the delicious meal was done, everyone looked at Greg, assuming he would be first to speak, but they were in for a surprise. Josh and Trace -- the students he brunched with earlier in the day -- approached the microphone and announced *they* would be hosting the show.

The program began with three tributes to the late friend after whom Greg named the Foundation's first scholarships. One of Bailey's relatives kicked things off by giving a speech about him. Then, a representative of the football camp where Greg and Bailey met a decade earlier went on stage and announced a plaque was being put up in the locker room -- a plaque that talked about life being about more than just winning games.

Finally, a representative of the college Bailey planned to attend a decade earlier had he lived went on stage and announced that the school decided to create and fund a special one time scholarship and name it after Bailey -- *and* they were going to let Greg pick the winner of it, even though they had never even met him before.

It seemed to be an amazing leap of faith -- the audience was shocked -- but it would be just one of many surprises to come.

After the crowd settled down, Trace said it was time to pay tribute to the supporters who helped make the Foundation a success. Everyone expected a bunch of wealthy donors to get called up on stage, but that wasn't what occurred. Greg had decided the awards would be given to people who usually aren't appreciated in public -- like the lady who printed the Foundation's first business cards and the accountant who helped with all the financial work. Not overlooking the people who are usually over-looked, it was a reflection of the lesson Greg learned as a boy -- treat everyone you meet like they came into your life for a reason.

After a few more awards and grants were handed out, it was revealed that the next surprise was for Elliott, the long-time Brunch Bunch Kid who caught the foul ball at his first pro baseball game.

The principal of a highly selective high school -- a high school that turned Elliott down when he applied two years earlier -- approached the microphone and explained to the audience that Greg had recently been a guest speaker at their school.

"In the weeks that followed," she explained to the audience, "a number of our students got to join The Brunch Bunch, and as a result, many of them met Elliott. And one by one, they returned to campus and said the same thing: The school would be an even better place with Elliott in it."

The principal paused, smiled and said, "And we agree."

Two years after Elliott was rejected, the high school he dreamed of attending not only let him in -- they gave him a full scholarship to boot.

As Elliott leapt on stage and hugged the principal, Greg watched on with pride. It was a moment that showed the true potential of the network he created. Make no mistake, there was nothing unique about people using their connections to help a friend. In fact, it occurs every day. What *was* unique was that, in this case, the people doing it were teenagers and the friend they were helping was from a different race and background.

It wasn't changing the game -- just who gets to play.

After Elliott sat down, the co-hosts returned to the podium and said it was time to do what everyone was waiting for -- give out the Foundation's first ever scholarships.

Suddenly, right on cue, the double doors to the banquet room opened and three students walked in, each one holding a Milkshake Trophy.

While most of the guests were distracted by the look (and smell) of the unusual trophies, the people who served as scholarship judges were surprised by something else -- the *number* of them. There were only scheduled to be *two* scholarships, but there were *three* trophies.

Harvard Charlie leaned over to his date and whispered, "I don't know what's up Greg's sleeve, but some kid in this room is in for a *big* surprise."

Charlie was right. And after the first two scholars were honored, Rocky went on stage to unveil it.

As the audience watched on, the kid in the tux peeled the sticker off the front of the third and final trophy and discovered the surprise Scholar was someone he had known all his life. *Himself.*

According to the co-hosts' copy of the script, that was the grand finale. So, while Rocky's mom sobbed with joy, Trace and Josh approached the podium to thank everyone for coming and say goodnight. When suddenly, Greg headed toward the stage to say something for the first time all night.

"Sorry to interrupt," he said, "but I think their script is missing a page or two because according to my copy, we're just getting started."

He paused, then added, "First up is the live auction. People kept telling me that every real gala has one, so we're gonna have one, too."

The audience sat up on the edge of their seats. What valuable item was going to be auctioned off to raise money? An exotic trip??? A diamond???

Uh, not exactly.

The "valuable item" turned out to be a framed copy of *Senior News* -- the magazine featuring Greg and his Grandma on the cover.

The audience started laughing loudly, but Greg insisted it was no joke.

"This isn't just any magazine cover, folks. This one is signed by the world's greatest Grandma!" he declared. "And if the world's greatest athlete's autograph is valuable, then the world's greatest Grandma's autograph is valuable, too! We start the bidding at five thousand dollars!"

Charlie later recalled, "I know that already seems nuts as it is, but I'd like to point out that his Grandma *didn't even sign her name.* Just the word *Grandma.* Think about it. It's like Babe Ruth signing something *Athlete.*"

Greg waited for someone to make the opening bid of five thousand dollars, but nobody even bid a buck. You could've heard a pin drop. The excitement building all night had come to a sudden and awkward halt.

But Greg refused to budge.

It seemed like the silence was going to last forever, when suddenly, a complete stranger in the back of the room ran up to the podium, said he felt inspired by the night, wanted the autograph, and was willing to match the largest gift the Foundation had ever received -- $5,000 -- just to have it.

The entire room was shocked -- including Greg's Grandma, who hollered that the man was "crazier than Greg!" Little did she know, she hadn't seen anything yet. Her grandkid was *still* just getting started.

As soon as things calmed down, Greg said he had two more surprises.

Then, he suddenly turned to his right and surprised Josh, the co-host, with *a five thousand dollar scholarship.* And before anyone could catch their breath, he turned to his left and surprised Trace with one, too!

The audience leapt to their feet to give a standing ovation, while the boys' moms began sobbing like Rocky's mom had done moments earlier.

The scholarships for the co-hosts seemed like an incredible twist -- and certainly one that nobody saw coming. It also seemed to be the perfect ending -- but Greg declared he still had one more announcement to make. He said it had to do with his "immediate future."

He took a deep breath, then told everyone how he promised his parents that he'd go to law school after he sent a kid to college. It seemed like he was giving a farewell speech, until suddenly, he began telling the crowd how he'd been denied access to a restaurant earlier in the day and how that proved there was still much more work to be done.

He took another breath, looked at his mom and dad, shrugged his shoulders and said, "So, I'm sorry, but I just can't walk away yet."

Greg's parents looked like they were going to faint, but believe ir or not, their son still had one more surprise up his sleeve.

And it was the biggest one yet.

When the room quieted down, Greg asked all of the students who were *not* there to get scholarships to rise -- there turned out to be fifteen in all.

He told them he was setting up criteria based on attendance, GPA, conduct and civic service, and that each of the fifteen who could meet that criteria would get $5,000 for college -- a staggering $75,000 in all!

And then, and only then, Greg smiled and said the show was over.

As the crowd headed toward the exits, still reeling from all the twists and turns, Charlie approached his old pal to get some answers.

"You were denied access to a restaurant?" he asked suspiciously.

"Can you believe that?" Greg replied.

"What restaurant was it?" Charlie asked, convinced there was a catch.

"Keyser's Place," Greg said matter-of-factly.

It was just as Charlie figured.

He wagged his finger at Greg and said, "You know what I think? I think you didn't want to walk away from all this, and you felt like you needed an excuse if your parents gave you a hard time about it, so this morning, you purposely went to the one restaurant where you knew you might get a hard time just so you could come here tonight and tell everyone that you've got to keep fighting the good fight. Getting turned away from a restaurant -- that wasn't a change in the script. It was *part* of it."

Charlie looked proud of himself for 'figuring out' what was going on, but Greg was not overly impressed. Like any director, he wanted to leave the audience with at least one question still unanswered. A plot twist -- *a cliffhanger* -- that would make them think. And even if Charlie did unravel that mystery, there was still another one that left him stumped...

How in the world would a substitute teacher come up with $75,000?

Amd how could Greg be so sure that Charlie didn't know the answer? Simple. *Because there wasn't one yet.* Truth be told, as Greg left Maggiano's, he had no idea how he was going to come up with the money.

"You have no plan?!" Charlie bellowed. "What are you going to do?"

"Well," Greg said sarcastically, "I figured what I would do is wait for a stranger to walk in the door and drop off the money."

Greg was only joking, of course. After all, how could he have possibly known that was *exactly* what was about to happen just a few hours later?

**

When Greg arrived home from the Gala, he was so tired that he headed straight to bed without even changing out of his suit.

At least, he *tried* to go to bed.

He had so many thoughts running through his mind that he was unable to sleep. Instead of continuing to toss and turn, he decided to put his shoes back on, go for a walk and get a milkshake. Three blocks down the road, he found a place that was still open, but they didn't have shakes on the menu.

As he turned to leave, a customer suddenly called after him.

"Hey," the man said, "My name is Lou. I'm a doctor. I go to the gym on weekends. You take those kids there every Sunday. Come meet my friend Maddie and tell her about what you do. She'd really be inspired."

Greg was tired, but he agreed to do as Lou asked (in return for a grilled cheese sandwich). After hearing the story, Maddie said she was *so* inspired that she wanted them to go with Greg for the shake right then and right there. When a waitress, Sugar, heard what was going on, she took off her apron and said she wanted to go with Greg for a shake, too!

Off they went, in the middle of the night, a doctor, an artist, a waitress and a substitute teacher in search of some milkshakes.

A few blocks down the road, they came upon a popular twenty-four hour restaurant called The Tempo Cafe and headed inside.

For the next thirty minutes, the four sat at a table laughing, joking and enjoying their milkshakes. As they did, Greg decided he wanted to keep some souvenirs from the night -- so he went over to the manager on duty and asked if he could keep the glasses they were using.

The manager, George, was in no mood to deal with a goofy customer so he turned down Greg's request and told him to go back to his seat. While Greg tried to change George's mind, a man walked in Tempo's front door and immediately thought Greg looked familiar. When he overheard the conversation about milkshake glasses, he suddenly put it all together.

"Milkshakes?!" he hollered. "That's why I recognize you! You and your friends take kids for milkshakes! I've read about you in the paper!"

The man was *so* excited to see Greg that he ran over to the table, sat in Greg's seat and *finished Greg's shake.*

Sitting around the table in the middle of the night at a twenty-four hour cafe, Lou, Maddie, Sugar and the complete stranger laughed and joked and gulped down the rest of the shakes without giving a single second's thought to the fact that they were from different races, cultures and backgrounds.

After watching with pride from a distance, Greg pulled up a chair and joined in the fun.

Shortly after four a.m., the five new friends finally went their separate ways. As he walked back to his apartment, four glasses dripping a trail of vanilla behind him, Greg was smiling from ear to ear. And not just because the day was one of the most incredible of his life. And not just because the manager at Tempo changed his mind and let him keep the glasses. No, he was smiling because a stranger had walked in the door out of nowhere and inspired him to come up with the idea that would help him raise all that money he had just pledge to raise. And this wasn't just any idea cooking in his head. He was absolutely certain it was the world's greatest idea ever.

And what was it?

Greg decided that if people were that excited to have a milkshake with him, he could *charge people five thousand dollars to do it.*

He figured it was a sure-fire way to come up with the money to fund those scholarships, but as word began to spread, most people thought his *foolproof idea* was actually nothing more than *proof he was a fool.*

And at first, they seemed to be right.

No matter how hard Greg tried, he couldn't sell a single $5,000 shake.

To add to his troubles, something else *was* sold -- the building where he lived. He was reluctant to pack up and move, but he soon began to see a silver lining. He spent nearly four years trying to change the world outside his window. Perhaps, a new apartment with a new window would give him a chance to take on a whole new set of challenges.

So, as soon as he moved in to his new place a few blocks away, he put the rocking chair by the window and began exploring his new view.

All the way to the left, he could see The Green -- the community where he spent much of his time teaching over the past several years. All the way to the right, he could see The Big Hotel -- one of the fanciest places in the entire city. There was less than a mile between the two, but Greg knew it might as well be a thousand. The world of The Green and the world of The Big Hotel rarely if ever merged together.

Almost instantly, Greg knew what he could do to change his new view for the better. Just as he tried to build a bridge between The Benches in Louisiana, and just as he tried to build a bridge between his own students from different backgrounds through the brunches, he now dreamed of building a bridge between The Green and The Big Hotel. To connect the dots on his left and on his right, to create an opportunity for the two worlds to co-exist together instead of just side-by-side.

He stayed up night after night plotting ways to make it happen, but it wasn't the only reason his new view kept him up late.

As fate would have it, Greg could also see the local movie theater out his new window and the theater's neon sign was a painful nightly reminder of the lifelong dream he was sacrificing to help the kids reach theirs.

Fortunately for Greg, there was great news to keep his spirits high. He sold his first $5,000 shake -- and to no less than NHL Star Chris Chelios.

The two drank them at Chris's annual charity golf outing.

Not surprisingly, a hockey legend drinking a $5,000 milkshake on a golf course made headlines in a bunch of papers. And the next thing you know, other people started ordering a $5,000 milkshake of their own.

A law firm ordered one for their boss for Christmas. A banker ordered a shake for his wife for Valentine's. And on and on it went.

Greg's milkshakes became so popular that a carpet company even used him in an advertisement. (According to the ad, Greg's Grandma hired the carpet company because Greg "won't sit at the table when he drinks his milkshakes and keeps spilling on my carpet.")

After a few months, Greg raised the price up to $7,500 per shake -- adding whipped cream to justify the increased cost. He seemed to be pushing his luck, but the orders just kept coming.

And each time Greg met one of the buyers for a shake, he saved their used glass so it could be turned into a trophy to go along with the scholarship that would be named after the person who bought it (or the company they represented, or one of their relatives if they drank the shake in someone's honor or memory).

As unlikely as it might've seemed when he first came up with the idea, so many people bought one of Greg's shakes that he was able to cover the scholarships he pledged to fund if any of those fifteen kids met the criteria he announced at Maggiano's -- and there was *still* money to spare.

And he knew exactly how he wanted to use the rest.

In the fall, he gave a college scholarship to Cliff, the kid from his old high school, and one to Fitz, the student who led the band.

**

While Greg's foundation blossomed, his physical condition continued to get worse. He was sleeping less which meant he was exercising less which meant the muscles were slowly starting to fizzle away. To top it off, his hair continued to fall out in clumps -- until, finally, he just shaved off what was left -- making his big ears stand out more than ever.

A year after being featured in magazines as a young, strong, healthy bachelor, Greg was suddenly bald, weak and exhausted. He tried his best to stay positive, but he found it harder and harder to look in a mirror and feel good about what he saw.

Determined to snap out of the funk, Greg came up with a way to get back in good shape and raise money for The Foundation at the same time. He announced plans to run in his first ever marathon -- collecting donations from supporters for each mile he ran, just as he collected them for each book he read when he was a boy.

His friends admired his goal, but they were not so sure he could do it.

"You've never run in a marathon," said Arthur, an experienced runner who lived one floor above him. "What makes you think you can do this?"

The answer was one Arthur probably should have seen coming.

"If Forrest Gump can run non-stop for a couple years," Greg explained matter-of-factly, "I think I can handle running a couple miles one time."

Obviously, it made no sense to think it was possible to complete a marathon without any training just because a made-up movie character ran non-stop for several years, and Arthur was going to try and explain that to Greg -- but the issue turned out to be moot.

A few weeks after pledging to make the 26.2 mile run, Greg had to have two more operations on his feet.

He was really depressed about the setback, but his Grandma didn't let him wallow in self-pity for long.

She huffed, "We've already been through this. If you gotta stay off your feet, just work on something you can do sitting down -- like your art."

He knew better than to argue with his Grandma, so he did as she instructed and got back to work on his drawings.

He also spent more time focusing on his logo.

Back when he first drew it, people thought the logo was "too simple." What they did not know at the time was that the logo had more than one meaning -- and even more than two. According to Greg, there was a *third* meaning. And, he decided, this was the perfect time to unveil it.

In Version One, the logo represented the things Greg saw outside his childhood window. In Version Two, it represented the different parts of The Brunch Bunch (BrunchBunch.com) program. Version Three was going to be all about scholarships -- *new* scholarships, to be exact.

In Version Three, *The Ladder* symbolized Greg's belief you should never underestimate the strength of those who help themselves up the ladder of success. With that belief in mind, the new Ladder Scholarship was going to assist students who were so busy working to, for instance, help their family pay the bills that their grades suffered a bit because of it. They only had B or C grades, but they clearly had a straight A work ethic.

The Tombstone represented Greg's philosophy that the only thing that lives forever is a legacy -- and that in order to leave one, you first must create one. With that in mind, The Legacy Scholarship was going to go to a student who was carrying on Greg's legacy: breaking barriers, building bridges and making a difference at a young age.

The Three Ovals once again depicted three milkshake glasses. But this time, instead of representing the day Greg took two kids for shakes and the woman sitting next to them moved her purse, they symbolized the Milkshake Glass Trophies that were going to be given to the new Scholars.

Greg intended to get to work creating the other two pieces of the puzzle -- the scholarships based on *The Triangle* and *The Silhouette Man* -- but his schedule was so packed that it was difficult to find the time to do it.

And then, September 11th happened.

On September 11, 2001, America suffered one of the worst attacks ever. That Friday, anxious to get away from the TV coverage he watched all week long, Greg accepted an invitation to attend a special service promoting peace and harmony. Afterwards, he went out with five of the other people there -- four of whom he didn't know.

Not surprisingly, they talked about the terrorist attacks while they ate -- it really was an impossible subject to avoid. What made their conversation unusual, though, was that instead of dwelling on what happened, they were talking about what could be done *in response.*

One of the people, a young building developer named Jonathan, was thinking about it from a real estate perspective. What could be built on that space where the Trade Centers stood to prove the nation was still standing? Greg, on the other hand, was thinking about the kids. What could be done to show them that you can turn anything -- even something *this* negative -- into something positive?

By the time the bill came, the two young men who had never met before decided to try and find a way to combine their two ideas. The plan they came up with was a contest where high school students would create designs to rebuild the space where the Trade Centers stood, then write essays explaining how their designs captured the strength people in New York were showing in the aftermath of September 11.

The idea was well-received.

A teacher named Mr. Mack said, "I always tell students that a building, if you do it right, can tell a powerful story. This was a chance for them to do exactly that -- design buildings that tell powerful stories."

It was also a chance for them to go to college.

The students who won the contest were going to receive The 11-10-02 Foundation Mountain Scholarships -- named after the mountain in the logo and representative of the idea that it is good to build something big and positive out of something negative.

**

In the weeks that followed 9-11, a number of schools invited Greg to speak to students about intolerance, diversity and dealing with tragedy.

One invitation brought him to Kentucky.

He looked forward to his first ever visit to the Bluegrass State, but under the circumstances, he wasn't too sure what kind of a response to expect. From his time in Louisiana, he knew how nice people in the South could be, but in the wake of such a horrible terrorist act, it would be very understandable if even the kindest of people were a little slow to roll out the welcome wagon for a visitor.

And yet, that's exactly what the people of Kentucky did.

When Greg got lost in his rental car, a woman didn't just give him instructions -- she gave him her map. When he asked a local resident where he should eat, she not only suggested a restaurant -- she went there with him so he wouldn't eat by himself. When he strolled into the local courthouse and asked if he could check his e-mail there, a man instantly rose from his seat and offered up his desk. It was only as Greg was leaving that he found out the man *was the judge.*

The way everyone welcomed a complete stranger with open arms would have made Greg feel good at any time, but to see them do it just days after 9-11 really was astounding.

As Greg wrote in a guest column for the paper at the end of his trip, "After what I experienced the last three days, I've reached a conclusion. The world would be a better place if everyone was a little more Kentucky."

While Greg was there, he also got the chance to spend time with Jarrett (from the Jefferson Awards) and his family.

Once again, the little boy with cancer put Greg's physical problems back into perspective. How could Greg complain about the pain in his feet when Jarrett only had one leg? How could Greg complain about being bald at the age of 28 when Jarrett looked that way since he was ten?

He also paid a visit to the hospital where Jarrett's organization brought toys to other sick kids. Seeing the program the boy put together in spite of all his obstacles, Greg was reminded yet again a person's *true* strength has nothing to do with how big and strong they seem on the outside.

That reminder helped give him the idea for the final new scholarship.

In Version Three of his logo, *The Silhouette Man* stood for the idea you should never measure a person's strength by the shape of their silhouette, or shadow. With that in mind, the Silhouette Scholarship was going to help a student who achieved great things despite having to deal with physical obstacles along the way -- a kid whose true strength came from within.

The boy from Kentucky was not the only student helping out the community at a young age. Clifford -- the student from Greg's old high school -- was trying to make a difference, too.

On his very first day of college, Cliff went for a walk and found a local grade school where he could volunteer. Over the next few months, he returned to the grade school on a regular basis and began bringing his new college classmates with him. It turned out he was literally trying to trace the civic steps Greg took during his freshman year a decade earlier.

Before long, university officials found out about what Cliff was doing. They were proud of him and curious about what inspired him. When he told them about Greg's speech at his old high school, it was not long before they invited Greg to come speak to *their* students.

The speech at Cliff's college was scheduled for November 8, 2001.

Greg could have flown home the next day -- the 9th -- but as a way of showing Cliff that he admired his volunteer efforts, he decided to stay through the weekend and hold that week's brunch there.

And so, on Greg's 29th birthday, 11-10-01, Greg, Cliff and the others met up for brunch at a beautiful restaurant called Brasserie Les Halles. The "kids" were a handful of the ones Cliff was tutoring on a regular basis.

At first glance, it appeared to be like all the previous brunches. Adults and students eating a great meal and getting to know each other while they did it -- talking about college and careers, learning about diverse cultures and backgrounds. But it was clearly no ordinary brunch. For instead of turning to the adults and asking them questions, Cliff was now *answering* questions that the kids were asking *him*.

Right before Greg's eyes, a student became a teacher.

In the process, by passing on the kindness, Cliff had brought the whole experience full circle. And, it turned out, that was all Greg was waiting to see. After 243 weeks in a row, his streak of brunches was over.

Cliff was stunned that he had inspired the end of such a long streak just by tutoring kids at a local school, but he really shouldn't have been that surprised at all. Whether it's making an effort to talk a classmate out of saying hateful things or picking one single brick up off the street or trying to find a place to bring a spare bag of bagels or getting shirts for one single school out your window or just tutoring one single kid, you can never underestimate the power of a simple act of kindness.

If the end of the streak of brunches was a fitting way to celebrate Greg's birthday, then the events of that night were icing on the cake.

Inspired by Greg's story, Cliff's roommate Perry decided he wanted to bring people of different cultures and backgrounds together, too -- and he decided Greg's 29th birthday was the perfect excuse to start doing it. So while Greg and Cliff were with the group at brunch that afternoon, Perry was calling all over the city asking people to come together that very night.

Perry's efforts were more successful than he could've ever hoped.

After the sun went down, *forty complete strangers* -- students from five different local universities -- gathered together on just a few hours notice to celebrate the birthday of a guy they didn't know.

Cliff laughed, "Some of them even ran out and got birthday gifts and birthday cards.... *they had never even met him.*"

Greg was overwhelmed by their efforts, and particularly touched by the restaurant that was chosen -- a place called John Harvard's.

"We would've taken you to the actual university," Perry said with a grin, "but that was a little bit out of our budget."

For two hours, the forty students of different races and backgrounds set those differences aside and made new friends. And when the event was over, the students presented Greg with a special gift.

A menu.

That's all it really was -- just a menu -- but there was no telling Greg that. As everyone went their separate ways, he clutched that menu with the word *Harvard's* across the front like it was as important as an actual diploma bearing the same name. And that's because, to him, it was.

**

As word spread that The Brunch Bunch Streak ended, people began to tally up the statistics -- such as the fact that over 700 people from 32 different states and six different continents had attended at least one of the brunches -- but more than any other number, it was the *length* of The Streak that caught people's eye.

Greg was *twenty-four years old* the day he took two kids for shakes and *twenty-nine* when he took a break 243 weeks later. A commitment of time that was impossible to deny -- and almost impossible to imagine.

As one kid, Trace, pointed out, "I graduated from middle school, went to high school, graduated high school and went to college and the man had *still* never missed a single week of brunch. It was really pretty amazing."

The pats on the back were well-deserved, but the more compliments Greg received for maintaining The Streak for such a long period of time despite all the obstacles in his path, the more he seemed to believe he could overcome *any* obstacle without *any* help from *anyone*.

Then, one night, he was humbled back to reality...by a camera.

Greg and his friend, Guy, had gone to see Elliott play basketball at his new school. After the game, Greg went on the court to take a picture with Elliott, but unfortunately, the camera wouldn't work.

"Want some help?" asked Guy, who happened to be a photographer.

"I can do it," Greg said snidely. "It's a camera, not rocket science."

Guy watched with amusement as Greg shook the camera, pushed its buttons, checked the lens, then shook it again -- getting more and more frustrated until, finally, he gave up and declared the camera unfixable.

Guy chuckled softly, casually yanked the aluminum flip-top off of Greg's soda can, inserted it in just the right place in the camera and said, "Say cheese."

Greg laughed him off, insisting that could not *possibly* do the trick.

But, sure enough - FLASH - it worked like a charm.

It turned out the piece of the camera that covers the batteries had fallen off and there simply needed to be a substitute of some kind to hold the batteries firmly in place and act as a conductor of the current.

In the process of finding that substitute and inserting it in just the right place, Guy not only solved the problem -- he taught Greg a valuable -- and humbling -- lesson to remember in the future.

(25) Life is a challenge, but it is not an exam.
It is okay to ask for help from someone who knows more than you.

People thought the end of The Streak meant Greg might finally take a vacation, but now that schools were nominating students for the new scholarships, he wanted to get to work lining up judges to pick the winners. So, he spent his first brunch-free weekend in nearly five years with his Grandma, but then it was right back to volunteering.

The Legacy Scholarship Judging Panel was the easiest to assemble. Given the personal nature of the scholarship -- the fact that it was going to be given to a student who was carrying on the legacy Greg was trying to leave -- he decided to select the winner himself. For the other three kinds of scholarships (The Ladder, The Mountain and The Silhouette), he decided to line up thirty judges -- ten for each panel -- to pick the winners.

At first, he planned on asking some friends to volunteer to do it, but one single phone call from Lambert G. Wakefield changed all that.

Some time earlier, Greg read an article in which the very well-known CEO described himself as someone who stayed humble despite his great success and always made time to help others.

Having learned his lesson about not asking for advice, Greg eagerly looked up Wakefield's office number to set up a meeting. But each time he called, the CEO's assistant turned him away -- saying her boss was in a meeting, out of town, or just plain unavailable.

Finally, one time Greg called, the assistant said his timing was perfect. "Stay by the phone, and he will call you in two minutes," she said.

Greg excitedly paced back and forth, rehearsing all the questions he wanted to ask. Right on cue, the phone rang -- but before Greg could ask a single question, the CEO made a statement of his own.

"You should have taken the hint. I don't talk to people your age."

Greg tried to respond, but it was too late.

Mr. Wakefield had already hung up.

(26) Never make a hero out of someone you do not know.
Admire only the qualities within them about which you are certain.

Determined to turn a negative into a positive, Greg vowed he would prove that Mr. Wakefield was the exception and not the rule -- that most big-time executives *were* willing to lend their time and wisdom to support the efforts of young people. Greg said he would prove this by looking up the names of very successful people, tracking down their phone numbers and convincing them to serve on one of his new Scholarship Boards.

Greg's friends understood why he was upset, but they insisted he was only setting himself up for more disappointment. They said most powerful executives would never take his call let alone agree to give their time to help out a tiny foundation run by a substitute teacher they had never met.

Greg always replied the same way.

"Apparently, you've never heard of Brantley Foster."

Brantley Foster was a young college graduate working in the mailroom of a big company in New York, until he convinced a bunch of top execs to back his ideas -- at which point, he took over the entire company.

It was an inspiring example for Greg to follow. Of course, there was just one little problem -- Brantley Foster didn't actually exist and neither did the big-shots who supported his ideas. They were all just characters in a movie. But, as always, that mattered little to Greg. If Brantley could win over the top executives around town, then he figured he could, too.

(A belief that he felt even more strongly about thanks to a note of encouragement from Mr. Landers, the guy who let Greg take The Brunch Bunch to his health club -- a note that read simply: THINK BIG)

And so, despite the doubters, Greg moved forward with his plan.

As expected, some of the business leaders he called turned him down and others never replied at all -- but it didn't faze him one bit. He took the rejections in stride and just kept making more calls.

And the persistence eventually paid off.

One by one, a few started saying yes. And then a few more. And then a few more after that. When all was said and done, the young substitute teacher had shocked just about everyone by convincing thirty of America's most successful businessmen and women to join his team.

Mr. MacMillan, the head of a major toy company who was among those who signed on board, said, "Was it the largest charity on Earth? Of course not. But as someone who started from nothing, I don't care about that. All I care about is work ethic and passion. I don't worry about how old you are or how small your project is. If you have work ethic and passion, you'll have my respect."

Once MacMillan and the others were on board, Greg divided them up into three smaller groups -- one to select the Ladder Scholars, one to choose the Mountain Scholars and one to pick the Silhouette Scholar.

The meetings were scheduled for three Thursdays in a row in late May and early June. In the meantime, the nominees had a couple extra months to finish up their applications, and Greg had some extra time to make sure he planned out every last detail of the three Board meetings.

The decision to spend the extra time in that way was understandable -- these were going to be three very big meetings with some very prominent people -- but what he really needed to do was take a vacation.

He was *exhausted* -- to the point that he was having sudden sleeping spells. Sometimes, it was a cause for humor -- on one date, he fell asleep headfirst into her soup -- but it was usually much more serious -- one night, he collapsed in the shower, hitting his head and cutting it open.

And it wasn't just his body showing signs of wear and tear.

His rocking chair was, too.

In fact, Greg spent so many hours rocking in the chair that he *rocked a hole right through it* -- the splinters of the seat falling to the ground.

He was scared to tell his Grandma what happened to her chair, but she actually smiled when he broke the news. She called the splinters of the chair a "symbol of his work ethic" and told him to save them.

He did as she instructed -- framing them on his wall above his desk -- but he was still sad about what happened. The chair was much more than *just* a place to sit. Much like The Silhouette Man and The Ladder Horse from his childhood, that rocking chair had become *Greg's friend.*

Unfortunately, he didn't have much time to mourn his loss.

With all four scholarships created (The Legacy, The Mountain. The Ladder and the Silhouette) and the judges' meetings just around the corner, it was time to plan another party where the winners would be honored.

Given the success of the first event, Greg's friends said he should bring everyone back to Maggiano's -- but he had another place in mind.

The Big Hotel.

He loved everything about that event at Maggiano's, but a number of people still teased him every time he referred to it as a *Gala* -- "It was a banquet," they insisted. "Restaurants host banquets. Hotels host Galas."

Greg knew he should pay them no attention, but he just couldn't help himself. He wanted to prove he could put on a *real* Gala like sophisticated socialites do. He wanted to prove he could be *one of them*. And he was certain that a successful event for 500 people in the 10,000 square foot Regal Ballroom at The Big Hotel would silence all the doubters for good.

And what's more, like he dreamed when he first moved into his new apartment, he wanted to build a bridge between The Green on his left and The Big Hotel on his right -- and this seemed like just the chance to do it.

His friends admired his desire to think big, but the idea of having an event at The Big Hotel seemed like an awfully big step for the substitute teacher with the tiny foundation, and they doubted he could pull it off.

Greg insisted he was up to the challenge and wasted no time trying to prove it. In just a matter of days, he got a new website to promote the night, he lined up Kinko's as the evening's title sponsor and persuaded a local magazine to help publicize it.

As for the event itself, to make sure it ran smoothly, Greg created a Planning Committee comprised of a dozen friends willing to volunteer their time. With their help, he was certain the event would be a piece of cake to pull off, but it soon became clear he had gone from one extreme -- refusing to ask a friend (the photographer) for help -- to another extreme -- demanding his friends on the Planning Committee devote every waking minute to helping him -- and the result was just as bad.

No matter what his friends on the Committee did, Greg wanted them to do more. No matter how much time they spent, he told them to spend more. And he didn't ask nicely, either. Day after day, he sent them angry notes and barked orders at them through the phone. He was so determined to reach his goal that he lost sight of the feelings of the people who were helping him do it. Not surprisingly, his approach left his friends feeling disrespected and unappreciated -- until, one by one, they started to quit. After just a few weeks, most of the Committee had disappeared.

It was a turn of events that helped Greg finally begin to come to grips with a lesson that he should've learned a long time earlier when his angry notes burned down one bridge after another after another.

(27) How many people are on your side when you set a goal
is much less important than how many are still there when you reach it.

While Greg focused his attention on the event where the new Scholars were going to be honored, others focused their attention on him.

In the summer, Zeta Beta Tau honored him as its Man of Distinction. In the winter, he was honored as one of America's Daily Points of Light. President Bush and his father, President Bush, both sent letters saluting him for receiving the special honor given to just one American each day.

As the honors continued to pile up, the invitations to speak did as well.

In the spring, he was invited to speak at the Graduation Ceremony at Prairie State College. At the event, the community college planned to give Greg an honorary degree -- making him the youngest person in the school's history to ever receive one.

For Greg, it was especially meaningful because, honorary or not, this would be the first college diploma he ever actually held in his hands.

Mark rolled his eyes as he listened to his son go on and on about this honorary degree as if it was as meaningful as a real one.

He griped, "All these years later, the kid still couldn't figure out the difference between what was real and what was not."

Despite his father's grumblings, Greg continued to treat the event like it was going to be his actual college graduation. When PSC officials told him the graduation speaker always wears a special set of colors around the neck to recognize where he or she went to college, Greg said he did not want to wear any colors at all.

"Just the cap and the gown like my fellow graduates," he insisted.

As the day drew near, Greg got more and more excited. He requested tickets so he could have some people in the audience cheering him on just like the "other graduates" were going to have. The school granted the request, but unfortunately, his parents and sister were all unable to go and his Grandma said she was too ill to make the trip.

Determined to still put the tickets to good use, Greg invited some of his Foundation's Scholars to take their place.

Graduation Day - Prairie State College

While the five 11-10-02 Foundation Scholars took their seats in the back row, Greg took his seat up on stage. Decked out in his cap and gown, (with his mismatched socks peeking out the bottom), he looked around at the auditorium full of people and smiled from ear to ear.

It was *exactly* as he'd always dreamed.

Halfway through the ceremony, the President of Prairie State College, Dr. McCarthy, went up to the podium to introduce Greg.

It was a traditional introduction for a ceremony of that nature -- talking about the graduation speaker's accomplishments and the awards he had received -- until Dr. McCarthy mentioned something that took the audience -- and especially the five Foundation Scholars -- by surprise.

This was the first college graduation Greg ever attended in his life.

He not only skipped his own -- *he'd never been to anyone's.*

When the introduction was over, Greg took a deep breath, rose from his seat, approached the microphone and began his speech. He didn't have a single note to guide him, but he didn't need any. This was a moment he pictured since he was a boy.

He began by telling his "fellow graduates" about his lifelong effort to draw, and what his Grandma told him about straight lines when he was little. And then, he reflected on the struggles and obstacles he faced to get to this moment and this stage -- how it turned out his life had not been much of a straight line, either.

"But," he concluded, "the thing is, knowing what I know now, I don't regret it, because my Grandma was right. A straight line is the shortest distance between two points, but it's definitely *not* the most rewarding."

He paused for a moment to let his words sink in.

As they did, he asked The 11-10-02 Foundation Scholars in attendance to stand. As 2,000 people turned around to look at the five students in the back of the auditorium, Greg told them how proud he was to have them there and how important it was that they "cross a stage just like this one" some day down the road.

And then, he turned his attention back to the graduates sitting up front -- men and women who worked so hard to reach this moment in their lives. He told them to be as proud of the obstacles they overcame as they were proud of the goals they achieved. And, he said in conclusion, he hoped they were as proud to be a part of the graduating class as he was.

When he finished his remarks, the audience rose to their feet to applaud him. Dr. McCarthy later said it was the first standing ovation he'd ever seen for a graduation speaker in his time at Prairie State.

In a normal situation, with the speech complete, the presentation of the honorary degree would come next. Before the event, though, Greg begged school officials to make an exception and let him line up with the graduates so that he could do what he'd never done -- *cross the stage.*

The graduation planners granted his unusual request, but didn't want to mess up the alphabetical order of the graduates, so they told Greg to just file in at the back of the line.

One by one, the students crossed the stage as Greg anxiously waited his turn. After all these years, and so many ups and downs, he was now just minutes away from holding a college degree for the first time.

Moment by moment, he inched closer, until finally, every name was called but his. Every graduate had crossed the stage but him. From where Greg stood, he could see them holding his diploma. It was now just a few precious feet away.

All he had to do was take those last few steps to get it.

And he did.

As the audience cheered him on and his name echoed through the rafters, Greg crossed the stage, took his degree, hoisted it in the air and screamed with joy. The boy who once hoped to finish top in his class from the Ivy Leagues was now a thin, frail, limping, tired, bald man who had just graduated last in his class with an honorary degree from a community college, and yet, he'd never been happier in his entire life.

> *(28) What you're holding in your hand at the end of a journey is not as important as the walk you took to get there.*

After the event, Greg took the photos to his Grandma's apartment. These were the pictures he promised her six years earlier.

As soon as he arrived, he began excitedly flipping through the stack -- giving his Grandma a play-by-play description of each picture as he did.

"This is me in my cap and gown before I went on stage! And this is me giving my speech! And this is me getting the degree!"

It was *such* a perfect moment that Greg wished it could go on forever -- but he knew that, eventually, it had to end. After all, the Scholarship Boards had their meeting in just a few, short days. And as with everything in Greg's life, there had been a bump in the road that required his attention.

The problem was that the executives who agreed to serve on the three Scholarship Boards were *so* busy that there was just no way their schedules would allow them time to review all the nominees' applications.

It seemed to be a real dilemma, but Greg came up with a solution. He decided to create a *Junior* Scholarship Board responsible for going through the nominees and selecting the finalists. That way, when the three Scholarship Boards met, they only had to review ten nominees apiece.

Everyone liked the idea -- until Greg announced the Junior Board would be *a bunch of teenagers.*

The decision to give young people this opportunity struck many as a big mistake -- "You can't trust a bunch of kids with something like this!" one skeptic said -- but Greg disagreed. As far as he was concerned, the idea was not only consistent with his goals -- it *was* his goal. To prove young people can do a great job if they're just given the chance to do it.

And so, despite the critics, he moved forward with the plan -- rounding up a dozen students from a dozen schools to serve on the Junior Board.

When the time came, the group met in a back room at a local restaurant and began reviewing the applications. Two teens from Greg's hometown -- a girl named Chrissy and a boy named Alex -- were put in charge. Despite the doubters, the group took its role seriously. In fact, they took it so seriously that their meeting lasted well past one in the morning.

With the finalists selected, it was time for the Senior Boards to meet. The Ladder Board went first.

At precisely ten minutes past six, Greg walked into the spacious conference room where the ten executives were gathered, took his seat at the head of the table and said in the most confident of voices, "Ladies and gentlemen, it's time for us to get down to business."

Decked out in a perfectly-pressed suit, a handful of America's most successful leaders sitting along either side, for one fleeting moment, the substitute teacher looked and felt like a *real* CEO.

But after crossing the stage with the students of Prairie State, it no longer mattered to him quite so much if anyone else saw him that way.

He no longer wanted to be *one of them*.

He wanted them to be *one of us*.

And it was right about then that everyone noticed something quite unusual hanging up on the wall. It was Greg's BOARDROOM sign -- the very same one he hung up years earlier in the Lunch Lady's room at Blue Academy. He brought it to the meeting and put it up on the wall before the Board Members arrived.

"I wasn't stepping into their world. They were stepping into ours," Greg said with pride, when asked why he brought the sign with him.

Seven days later, the Mountain Scholarship Board had its meeting, and seven days after that, the Silhouette Scholarship Board took its turn. And each time, the BOARDROOM sign was hanging on the wall.

As the final meeting came to an end, Greg walked out the door with a feeling of great satisfaction. With the applications reviewed and the judges' votes cast, he was now *thisclose* to fulfilling the third version of the logo.

With his civic goal so close to being achieved, Greg started thinking more than ever about his Grandma. He knew he never would have been able to get so far without her support. After all, she was the one who gave him that chair and made him believe a substitute teaching restaurant doorman could build a foundation from scratch. The one who taught him how to deal with rejection. The one who urged him to work twice as long as the kids who seemed twice as smart. The one who convinced him it was okay if he couldn't draw straight lines.

Day after day, for nearly three decades, Greg's Grandma had been there for him. It might have been *tough love*, but it was love all the same.

In return, Greg repeatedly tried to show his appreciation. Over the years, he arranged everything from a surprise party for her birthday to autographs from her favorite TV stars like Regis Philbin. And yet, Greg always felt like he still had not done enough to thank her. He really did want her to understand that she was the World's Greatest Grandma.

Whenever he told her that, she wagged her finger and said, "That's what *you* think. You go ask ten other kids, and you'll get ten other answers. Everybody who's got a Grandma will say their Grandma is the best one."

Greg nodded politely, but her words did little to sway him. He knew there were millions of *really great* grandmothers, but as far as he was concerned, *his* Grandma was truly in a league all her own -- and no matter what it took, he wanted to convince her of that.

And then, just a few days after the Scholarship Board meetings, Greg came up with the perfect way to do it.

His plan was to create a website, www.WorldsGreatestGrandma.com, which would host a "competition" to find the *WorldsGreatestGrandma*, except that there would be just one judge -- *him*.

The contest was obviously a farce, but there was no telling Greg that. He insisted he would be a "fair" judge and moved forward with the plan.

A few days later, he created the website. Then, he submitted a one page essay to nominate his Grandma. A minute later, he declared the "competition" closed. A minute after that, the judging panel (himself) read the (only) nomination and selected the winning Grandma (his own).

Charlie laughed, "How was that *possibly* fair?"

"The judges considered every essay fair and square," Greg shot back.

Charlie started pointing out the obvious -- *there was only one essay and it was the judge who submitted it* -- but Greg was too excited to care. In fact, he was so proud he thought he was going to *burst*. He *could not wait* to see the look on his Grandma's face when he told her that whether she liked it or not, she was, *officially*, the *WorldsGreatestGrandma*!

But he never got the chance.

Just a few hours later, that very day, she passed away.

Charlie said, "Every time Greg was about to celebrate reaching a goal, something went wrong. It happened to him more times than I could count, and at some point, it just became part of who he was. Hopelessly jinxed. Even he was able to laugh about it a little after it kept happening. But this one -- his Grandma passing away an hour before he went to see her to tell her about the contest -- this one seemed almost too cruel to be true."

Indeed, Greg had never felt anything so painful in his entire life. The sadness and grief caused by her loss and its timing was so all-consuming that he couldn't think straight.

Hoping to clear some of the thoughts from his head, he sent an open letter about his Grandma to his friends and wrote a guest column about her for *Senior News*. He was just trying to vent his feelings about her loss, but as fate would have it, by taking the time to do it, the single most negative experience of his life gave birth to something positive.

In the days that followed, people all over the country began responding to what he wrote about his Grandma. Some of those responses included donations to the Foundation in her honor.

When Greg took a moment to add up all the checks, he suddenly realized there was enough there to fund an entire extra scholarship.

A few days later, he met with his Grandma's caretaker on a bench behind the building where his Grandma had lived for the past decade. For twenty minutes, the two sat quietly, gulping down milkshakes and toasting the creation of this new and unexpected scholarship.

**

Greg would feel the pain of his Grandma's death for years to come, but in the short term, he distracted himself by focusing on the Gala at The Big Hotel. It was shaping up to be a real night to remember.

Four tables worth of items had been lined up for the night's silent auction. A bunch of great companies had signed on as sponsors. And thanks to the title sponsor, Kinko's, there were even going to be invitations this time around -- *thousands* of them.

Ironically, all the invitations created a new problem. Somebody had to stuff, seal and stamp all the envelopes.

Fortunately for Greg, a bunch of students volunteered. He was grateful for their help, but one kid in particular stuck out from the others.

A few months earlier, A.C. Lucas had been nominated for one of the Ladder Scholarships, but the Board did not pick him. A big, tough football player, A.C. hardly seemed the type to take defeat with a humble smile, and yet, here he was, offering to help with the invitations for the party honoring thestudents who were picked for the scholarships instead of him.

Knowing firsthand how hard it was to cope with rejection as a high school senior, Greg wanted to do something special for A.C. -- so he gave him two free tickets to the Gala. Even though he was just going to be a part of the audience, A.C. was so excited that he said he'd get there early.

A.C. was not the only one looking forward to the big event.

A week before it took place, Elliott gave a good luck gift to his former substitute teacher.

Elliott smiled and said, "It's the foul ball I caught at that game you took us to. That was five years ago now, but I've kept it all this time, and now I want you to have it. It'll bring you confidence next week."

"But what about you?" Greg asked.

"I'm about to graduate high school, and I'll be going to college in the fall. I've got all the confidence I need."

After years of dreaming and months of planning, the big night at The

Big Hotel finally arrived. At a quarter to six, hundreds and hundreds of people began parading inside the Regal Ballroom to find their seats.

Just as Greg pictured it, the event served as a bridge that united people from both sides of the tracks. Residents from The Green, CEOs of large companies -- for one night, they all were coming together under one roof.

As they stepped inside the ballroom, the supporters who had been around since the beginning could not believe how much the Foundation had grown. But if they were concerned things would change as they grew, those concerns quickly went away.

The Gala was still clearly going to be the *kids'* night to shine.

The centerpieces were milkshake glasses painted by students at Blue Academy. Fitz and his friends were once again playing the music. Instead of bringing in some celebrity, Greg tapped Rocky -- the 'kid in the tux' at the first gala -- to be the night's special guest speaker. Once again, a couple of teens had been chosen to host the show -- this time around, it was Cliff and two girls, Brandie and Hannah. And Greg was still, well, *Greg.*

He showed up to the event three hours early -- which was good -- *but he was wearing his pajamas.*

"I wasn't thinking about what to wear. I just didn't want to be late," he said with a shrug before rushing home to change while everyone ate dinner.

After dinner, the program began with the presentation of awards to a few of the Foundation's supporters. Once again, people thought the awards would go to some well-tailored executives. Once again, they were wrong.

Just like at Maggiano's, the awards went to supporters who usually get overlooked (like the man who made the trophies). There was also an honor lined up for The Lunch Lady and her two co-workers -- dinner for three at one of the nicest restaurants in the entire country.

With the awards handed out, they moved on to the scholarships.

The first was the one created and funded in memory of Bailey by the university he was going to attend had he lived. Greg was given the chance to select the student who would receive it, but in the end, he couldn't choose between two nominees. Luckily for them, the school decided Greg didn't have to pick -- agreeing to give a scholarship to each of them!

And the good news just kept coming.

A few moments later, it was announced that the Foundation was so proud of how A.C. handled rejection -- offering to help stuff invitations for the Gala -- that a brand new scholarship had been created just for him!

Then, it was Rocky's turn to be surprised (again). In the middle of his speech, he noticed the head of his university walking toward the stage. She said the school was so impressed by Rocky's freshman year that they were going to match the Foundation scholarship given to him last time!

With those surprises out of the way, it was time to give out the special scholarships to the kids who met Greg's challenge laid out at the first gala.

The challenge had been an amazing success. Of the fifteen students, three of them received jobs from people they met through the process. Another three received internships. Two got computers, and another eight received grants from the Foundation. To top it off, three of them managed to meet the challenge itself and earn $5,000 for college.

The parade of surprises and scholarships brought smiles to the faces of everyone in the room -- everyone except Greg. The man who pictured this night for years -- and scripted it all out right down to the final word on the final page -- was anxiously pacing in the back of the room. Like any director, he wasn't going to relax until the final curtain fell.

Next up was the live auction. This time around, Greg lined up some gifts *nobody* would laugh at -- a trip to France, a Total-Traveler cruise and a diamond to name a few -- and he recruited a savvy young business-woman to go on stage and auction them off to the highest bidders.

Once the auction was complete, it was time to give out the last set of scholarships -- the ones that represented the four symbols in Version Three of the logo. One by one, the scholarship winners were all called on stage.

The Legacy Scholarship was first. It went to Elliott. The Foul Ball Kid was indeed well on his way to becoming a College Man.

The Ladder Scholars were honored next, and then the Mountain Scholars took their turn -- their post-9/11 designs on display for all to see.

After the Legacy, Ladder and Mountain Scholars were honored, there was just one thing left to do -- reveal who was standing on top of the mountain in the logo. It was time to give out The Silhouette Scholarships.

The first was named after Jarrett. The boy from Kentucky was living proof a person's strength couldn't be measured by their size or shape. The scholarship went to a young man named Dennis, who graduated high school with all A's despite being confined to a wheelchair.

The second Silhouette Scholarship was named after Greg's Grandma. Despite being unable to walk or see in her final days, she had remained as strong as ever. The scholarship went to a young man named Dan. Despite a horrible accident that shortened his arms and forced him to spend his life on crutches, he managed to graduate high school at the top of his class.

Dennis and Dan were exactly what Greg pictured when he created the Silhouette Scholarship. The two boys had a level of confidence and strength that shattered any stereotype about so-called *handicapped* kids. And as the two boys basked in the glow of their inspiring acceptance speeches, the audience rose to their feet and gave them a standing ovation.

The Silhouette Scholars had been honored.

The picture was complete -- or so it seemed.

As Hannah, the co-host, stepped forward for the show's conclusion, a young man suddenly ran on stage with a Milkshake Trophy and declared there was a third Silhouette Scholarship to give out.

As if in slow motion, Hannah peeled off the sticker covering the base of the trophy. Sure enough, it was *her* name engraved on the front.

Her hands and legs began to shake, as she approached the microphone. "I, uh, oh my gosh, wow, I just can't...I just don't...I mean, I, uh...."

The surprise had left her -- literally -- speechless.

The audience was clearly touched, but they were also confused. The Silhouette Scholarship was *supposed to be* for students like Dennis and Dan who dealt with physical obstacles. Hannah, on the other hand, with her tall thin frame, pearly white smile and long flowing blonde hair, looked like a *cheerleader*. The *last* thing she looked like was a Silhouette Scholar.

But *that* was the point.

Hannah looked fine because her physical obstacle was *inside*. As a young girl, she had an operation on her heart that forced her to spend much of high school studying from home. So, her obstacle might have been hard to see, but it was certainly real. And just like Dennis and Dan, Hannah had not let her obstacles stop her from success -- graduating near the top of her class despite what she endured.

The image of the Silhouette was yet another irony in a story filled with them. The man standing on top of the mountain in the logo with his arms raised in victory turned out to be three people instead of one. And one of them -- Dennis -- couldn't stand. One of them -- Dan -- couldn't raise his arms. And the third -- Hannah -- wasn't a man at all.

In the back of the room, the boy everybody once laughed at because of his wide-eyed dreams could now be found laughing loudest of all. It may have taken him nearly three decades, but as Dennis and Dan and Hannah stood on stage, Greg had done what people always said was impossible.

He made The Silhouette Man come to life.

And, in the process, *The First Thirty* had just taken on a whole new meaning. Because, when all was said and done, between the students honored at Maggiano's and the ones honored at The Big Hotel, Greg's Foundation helped its first thirty Scholars.

Perhaps even more ironic was the identity of the people who raised the money to fund the scholarship for Hannah. Unlike so many of the other scholarships funded by corporations, or at least by wealthy individuals, Hannah's scholarship was made possible by *a bunch of teenagers*.

The civic-minded students volunteered for months doing everything from baby-sitting to car-washing until they came up with enough money to fund two scholarships. The first was given to one of the Mountain Scholars earlier in the night. The second was the one for Hannah.

To many in the crowd, the teens' efforts were the highlight of the night.

As Greg's neighbor, Arthur, put it, "The Foundation had become very grown-up in many ways, but, at the end of the day, the name -- 11-10-02 -- represented Greg's belief that people under thirty could make a difference. Knowing that a bunch of teenagers funded this final scholarship, I think it brought the entire thing full circle. It was just a very, very cool moment."

Even more fitting, perhaps, was the fact that the teenagers who did it were led by Alex. After serving on the Junior Scholarship Board and reading about the nominees, he wanted to help them to go to college -- hence, the decision to get some friends together and raise the money.

To many in the audience, that alone was enough to make Alex special -- but it turned out it wasn't the only reason the young man stood out.

A native of the same town where Greg and Charlie were raised, Alex appeared to have a great deal in common with both of them.

On the one hand, Alex shared Charlie's pursuit of life on the fast track to traditional success. He had already been accepted to the Ivy Leagues, was headed there in the fall, fully expected to land a high-paying job four years down the road -- and made no apologies for any of it. On the other hand, he was anxious to make a difference while he was young and even more determined to inspire his classmates to do the same.

Alex was not solely following Charlie's path to corporate America nor was he solely following Greg's path into the community. Instead, he appeared to be carving out his own path somewhere in the middle.

In the process, Alex became a living reminder that you don't have to choose between pursuing your dreams and helping others pursue theirs.

You can instead do a little of both and be a lot more balanced.

(29) If you want to conquer the world, you don't need to be 100% Charlie.
If you want to change the world, you don't need to be 100% Greg.
There is a middle ground. Find it.

With all the scholarships given out, Cliff approached the podium to thank everyone for coming and to remind them to drive safely on the way home. As he did, he suddenly noticed Greg making his way toward the stage for the first time all night. History was about to repeat itself.

When he got to the podium, Greg said he was sorry for interrupting -- but the co-hosts' scripts were once again apparently missing a page or two because according to his copy, the show was just getting started.

He said the first surprise up his sleeve was another live auction.

"The cruise, the trip and the diamond auctioned off earlier were great," he said, "but the most valuable item of all, I saved it for last."

The audience was abuzz with excitement. What could be even more valuable than a cruise, a trip and a diamond? *A safari? A brand new car?*

Uh, not exactly.

It turned out to be the stitches of Elliott's foul ball.

Greg's ex-girlfriend, Sloane, cracked, "I was speechless. Greg didn't even frame the ball -- just the red, stringy stuff."

The audience started shaking their heads, but Greg said he was *serious.* He said the story behind the foul ball symbolized believing in yourself and seizing opportunities. He said this was *art,* and he insisted, it was worth more than the cruise, the trip and the diamond *combined.*

The ballroom rocked with laughter, but Greg did not care. He knew that all he needed was one person to believe in his vision and see the value he saw. And, sure enough, one person did.

"Five thousand dollars!" a complete stranger suddenly called out.

The room was in shock. Five grand for some red string? It seemed too good to be true. And yet, Greg was just getting warmed up.

"We have one other outstanding item to auction!" he bellowed.

Outstanding? Um, *ridiculous* might be a better way to put it.

The second item up for auction was a framed scrap of aluminum.

Guy, the photographer, laughed, "It was the flip-top from Greg's soda can that I used to get that camera to work -- *he had framed it!*"

Again, the audience laughed -- the thing was literally garbage -- and again, Greg was unfazed by the reaction -- insisting one man's garbage was another man's art. And he knew all he needed was one person out of 500 to agree with him to prove it. And sure enough, one person did.

"Five thousand dollars!" a man called out.

The audience was stunned by the man's generous offer.

And yet, to Greg, it was apparently not quite generous enough.

"Five thousand dollars?" he replied from the stage, with a completely straight face. "My Grandma's autograph went for five thousand dollars! A piece of red string just went for five thousand dollars! This is *aluminum!*"

The audience spun around to see the man's reaction -- many assuming he'd storm out in anger that his offer had been mocked -- but he never did.

To the contrary, the man was *such* a good sport that he *outbid himself.*

In the process, the scrap of aluminum sold for $8,000. It was not only more money than the cruise, trip and diamond *combined* -- the winning bid was the largest one-time donation the Foundation had ever accepted.

It seemed to be a perfect finale -- a reminder that people really will support your dreams if you believe in them enough -- but Greg was not done yet. With the success of the auction, his confidence was soaring.

He knew it was time to make the *really* big announcement -- the one he waited for more than a decade to make.

"I have a dream!" Greg suddenly declared.

The audience giggled at the words that made them think of the famous civil rights speech, but Greg didn't laugh with them. This was *The Dream.* The one hatched inside his mind when he was sitting on a mattress on the floor in Louisiana, with the poster of Dr. King watching over his shoulder.

And what was this *Dream* Greg kept secret for years?

He said his *Dream* was much like Dr. King's dream. A world of people of different races and cultures coming together...with just one little twist.

In Greg's Dream, everyone was drinking milkshakes.

The audience began to laugh even louder, but he insisted he was serious. His *Dream* was that the whole world go out for milkshakes. And the way he figured, it had to start somewhere and some day, so why not right here and why not today?

"And as we do it," he declared, "as we cross the street to go get shakes, I want you to talk to new people -- to make new friends along the way."

Hannah laughed, "It was the single craziest thing I'd ever heard. He wanted everybody to get up and leave the hotel right then and right there."

And everybody did.

Hundreds of people in suits and dresses -- White, Black, Hispanic, Asian, young, old, single moms and CEOs -- they all rose from their seats, followed Greg out of the Regal Ballroom, down the hall, out the door of The Big Hotel and across the street to the little milkshake shop. And along the way, they talked to the people walking on their left and on their right -- even if they didn't know each other.

It was *exactly* as Greg had dreamed.

As the night came to an end and people began to make their way home from the milkshake shop, Charlie walked up to his friend of twenty-five years and said, "It's not exactly how they taught us to do it in business school, but I have to admit, you had a vision and you made it come to life."

Greg smiled warmly. To hear Charlie acknowledge his way of doing things had value -- to hear Charlie admit maybe there was more than one right path to success after all -- meant a lot to the kid with no corner office.

But before Greg could say thanks, Charlie spoke again.

"There is still one thing I don't get. If the shakes were so important, why didn't you just have them delivered to us at the hotel?"

Greg smiled broadly and said, "Because it wasn't about milkshakes."

"But I thought you said --"

"It was about the walk, Charlie. It's always about the walk."

And that, indeed, was the moral of Greg's story -- the moral it took him nearly thirty years to understand. Whether you're trying to build a company, earn a college degree or just get a milkshake, it's the process of getting where you want to go that matters most. *That's* when you learn things -- on your way to getting where you want to go. It's not about *where* you go or what you get when you arrive that is of greatest importance.

It's the walk -- always the walk -- that matters most.

**

Now that Greg brought the streak of brunches full circle, sent thirty students to college and even realized the beginning of *The Dream*, some people suggested he take what little time was left until his thirtieth birthday to *finally* relax a little and take a much-deserved vacation.

Greg appreciated the thought, but he had a different idea in mind. Instead of coasting to the finish line, he wanted to use the weeks that remained to test the limits of everything he learned over the previous twenty-nine years and eight months of his life.

And he knew exactly how he wanted to do it.

Over and over again, Greg was told the most important parts of his life were not real. His backyard friends were not real. The people he admired in books and films were not real. The thirty dreams on his Idea List were unrealistic. He wasn't a *real* student at Froehmann Whitfield. The skeptics accused him of having muscles that weren't real. His room with the Lunch Lady was not a real office. His milkshake glasses were not real trophies. The event at Maggiano's was not a real gala. The things he auctioned off were not real art. The degree from Prairie State College was not a real one. Even the competition that declared his Grandma to be the world's greatest was called a farce.

Over and over and over again, for nearly thirty years, he heard the doubters say these things. And over and over and over again, he tried to prove them wrong. But now, he had a whole other goal in mind.

Instead of convincing people something had value -- that it was *real* -- could he convince them to believe in something that even he admitted was not? Could he convince people to see the value in something that *really* didn't exist? Could he convince them to literally see value in *nothing*?

To find out the answer, he said he was going to create a film premiere from scratch. He was going to line up a caterer and get posters made, and there would be newspaper ads and a billboard, too -- he could already picture all of it in his head -- and he vowed to get all the companies that would be involved to do their part *for free*.

It seemed like a difficult task, but there was an added wrinkle that seemed to change it from *difficult* to *impossible*.

There would not actually be a film.

Greg's friends insisted he was nuts. They said no company in its right mind would support the premiere of a film that did not exist.

Greg strongly disagreed. He said it didn't matter if there was a film. He said if a person believed in something strongly enough, then others would believe in it, too -- even if they knew it didn't exist. So, despite the doubters, he started calling companies to ask for their support.

"Wait a second," said one CEO. "You want my company to help you promote the premiere of a film that doesn't exist?"

"That's right," Greg said proudly. "There's no film. Not even a short one. There's zilch, nada, *nothing*! So whaddya say? Are you in?!"

Not surprisingly, the CEO said no, and he wasn't alone. But each time, Greg just shrugged off the rejection and kept making more calls. And, sure enough, within a few days, his efforts produced the results he wanted.

A top photographer named Vincent and a top graphic designer named Maria agreed to help Greg make the posters. Kinko's agreed to print hundreds of copies once they were done. The local paper agreed to run ads in the movie section to promote the event, and a company even agreed to put up a giant billboard right in the middle of town promoting the "film."

Maggiano's Little Italy and the Cripple Creek Brewing Co. agreed to provide food and sodas for the special reception that would take place at the "premiere." The Eli's Cheesecake Company agreed to send a special, giant cheesecake in the shape of a milkshake for dessert.

Greg's friends were stunned by what he put together, but they were

positively speechless after discovering where the event would take place.
At the movie theater.

Loews Cineplex Entertainment agreed to close it down for one night --
the night of Greg's thirtieth birthday -- to host the premiere of a film they
knew did not exist. And for the eight weeks leading up to the big night,
they even agreed to put the posters up in two dozen of their theaters right
alongside the posters promoting the real movies.

"How in the world did you get them to agree to do it?" Charlie asked.

Greg shrugged, smiled and said, "I asked nicely."

It all seemed too good to be true, but Greg was still not satisfied.

His non-existent movie needed an audience!

In a speech before several hundred supporters, Greg revealed the plans
for his thirtieth birthday. Everyone there seemed real excited, until he told
them there was just one small catch. There would not actually be any film.

The audience was amused and confused all at once.

Elliott said, "The reception with the stars before the premiere sounded
cool, except that, well, if there's no actual movie, then who are the stars?"

A reception with movie stars -- that has no movie stars -- didn't sound
too impressive, but there was no telling Greg that. To the contrary, he said
it was *so* great that tickets were going to cost $125 apiece!

Most of his friends thought he was *nuts.*

Greg's neighbor, Arthur, laughed, "This was the premiere of a film that
did not exist. He would've been lucky if people agreed to show up *for free.*
To charge people $125 to go?? He completely lost his marbles."

Arthur wasn't the only one who felt that way, but Greg didn't care one
bit. He knew that as long as he kept believing in his idea strongly enough,
then eventually other people would, too. And, sure enough, they did.

Slowly but surely, as ridiculous as it seemed, people started filling out
forms to buy tickets. In some cases, they bought as many as ten!

A local parent, Annie, one of the few who always told Greg to keep
chasing his dreams, was loving every second of it.

"It wasn't like he tricked anyone," she boasted. "They all knew there
was *no movie.* And yet, they were *still* ordering tickets."

It seemed like Greg could finally relax, but he said he was just getting
warmed up. Having now convinced all these companies and people to see
value in *nothing*, Greg was going to do what he always dreamed. He was
going to prove that something imaginary could become real. He was going
to make *nothing* come to life.

"What do you mean?" Charlie asked.

"I'm making a movie!"

The idea seemed to be Greg's nuttiest yet. He had just one hundred
days to learn how to make a movie, come up with all the equipment,
assemble a cast, shoot the footage, edit it all together and have it ready to
play on the night of 11-10-02.

It seemed impossible, but Greg assured his friends that it would all work out in the end -- pointing out that Roy Hobbs didn't try out for pro baseball until he was much older, and he still became a champion.

"Who?" Charlie asked.

"You know," Greg said, "Roy Hobbs. The guy in *The Natural*. He was going to be a pro ballplayer, but he got sidetracked and didn't get the chance to chase his dream until he was older. Just like me and making movies. I was going to do it when I was younger, but I got *sidetracked*."

And so it was, with a make-believe baseball player as his inspiration, Greg embarked on the project of a lifetime -- learning how to make a movie and making it -- in a hundred days.

If the goal seemed far-fetched, it seemed even more so when people found out what Greg planned to do with the film *after* 11-10-02.

Throw it away.

Greg said that one day, perhaps, he would tell the story of the first thirty years of his life, and maybe that would be seen around the world, but what he was about to spend a hundred days and nights making -- if he did get it done -- was just going to be a "rough draft" of a portion of the story, and it was only going to be seen one time -- the night of 11-10-02.

His friends couldn't understand the point of putting so much time and effort into something that would be seen by so few people.

Greg always responded the same way.

"Because it's the walk that matters most."

In the days that followed, despite his inexperience, Greg actually got off to an impressive start. He managed to line up film and cameras and access to a top-of-the-line studio where real productions were filmed, and he got two of his friends to help out and do the editing.

He also lined up an entire "cast." His friends, his students, the Lunch Lady, the accountant, the manager from the Tempo Cafe -- they all offered to take a turn in front of the camera to help turn Greg's dream into a reality.

As for the man himself, he was having the time of his life -- practicing his "Director" lines everywhere he went.

"Quiet on the set!" Greg hollered as he walked down the street.

"Action!" he blurted out in an elevator filled with strangers.

He even got his very own Director's Chair (Rocky, the kid in the tux, wrote *Director* on a piece of tape, stuck it on the back of a stool, smiled and said, "If it's a film to you, it's a film to me.").

Unfortunately, the honeymoon would not last long.

Greg's journey had always been riddled with roadblocks -- and these last hundred days would be no different.

The first day on the set, he nearly started a fire. Then, a camera temporarily disappeared. One day, an entire box of tapes was misplaced. The editing machine broke down twice. For three days, Greg filmed people without realizing he had not turned on their microphone.

And that's just what happened *on* the set.

Off the set, just like always, Greg's path was no straight line, either.

On one occasion, a truck rammed into his car while he was parked on the side of the road. A few weeks after that, he flew out of town to give a speech. On the way back, the driver took him to the wrong airport, and he was stranded a thousand miles from home. His apartment got so cluttered with boxes that, more than once, he slept underneath a counter at the 24 hour Kinko's down the street just so he could stretch out a little. He was eating so little that, with fifty days to go, he already lost nine pounds. And to make matters worse, just like always, he had to endure the doubters -- people who thought his grand dreams were out of whack.

"You have no business making movies. You ought to stick to helping kids," said one 'expert' who Greg tried to contact for help.

As the date drew near, things went from bad to even worse.

With less than thirty days to go until 11-10-02, Little Jarrett died. The brave boy from Kentucky finally lost his fight with cancer.

Despite all the setbacks and the grief -- and despite not having his Grandma to call for advice any more -- Greg refused to quit. He was determined to make his vision a reality. From time to time, the stress did get the best of him and he fired off another one of his angry, rambling notes, but more often than not, the lessons of the past thirty years -- lessons about hard work and teamwork and perspective -- carried the day.

To make sure he stopped losing track of equipment (let alone nearly setting it on fire), Greg had brought in a top film student named Chris to make sure it got done right. When the editing machine kept jamming, he turned to a top-level production company to lend a hand. And instead of giving up because some people wouldn't teach him anything, he found others who would. So, no matter what happened, Greg just rolled with the punches and stayed focused on his goal.

And eventually, it all paid off.

On the 98th night, Greg completed his task. He stuck the finished tape in an empty cereal box, headed home and waited for the big night to arrive.

The Movie Theater - November 10, 2002

With the name of Greg's one-night-only film -- 11-10-02.com -- up on the marquee, his friends and students came streaming into the theater where they enjoyed the reception with the "stars" of the film -- *themselves.*

Elliott laughed, "We wore dark shades and signed autographs. And not just the kids. The adults, too. For one night, we really did feel like *stars.* "

At precisely seven-thirty, with popcorn in one hand and soda in the other, the audience took their seats. A few moments later, the lights went out and the "film" began to play.

A critic would say what was shown that night was not very good, and that critic would be right. By any standard, it was an amateur production. A truly *rough* draft pieced together in a hundred days by a guy who didn't know what he was doing, with a cast that had no idea how to act.

But the audience didn't seem to care, and neither did Greg.

For in that theater on that night, if only for one night, he did what he always dreamed since he was a little boy -- he made the wall *come to life.*

And in the process, he told the exact kind of story he always vowed to tell. A story about underdogs. A story about someone who stuck up for others who were treated differently. A story about a world where it was okay to dream.

Best of all, thanks to the sponsors and all those ticket sales, the event was raising more money for the Foundation than any other night ever had.

In every sense, the night was perfect -- the ultimate way to spend the final night of a thirty year journey. Two minutes into the film, Greg already had tears running down both cheeks. And then, it got even better.

After the final credits rolled, the Principal of Blue Academy walked to the front, took the microphone and introduced himself to the audience.

For the next few minutes, Mr. Brooks talked about the efforts Greg made to help his school, his staff and his students over the years, and how they knew Greg sacrificed his own dreams along the way to do it.

He said his school was a small one, and there was never much they could do to express their gratitude to Greg. But, he noted, on this night -- 11-10-02 -- there was one special way they could say thanks. He said he'd heard that Greg's most deeply held dream all his life was to make films and to win an Academy Award for his very first one. And, he said, as fate would have it, that was the one dream he could help make come true.

Nobody seemed too sure what Mr. Brooks meant, but they started to figure it out when he smiled and said, "Because, you know, as the Principal of Blue Academy, I am, technically speaking, the head of *an Academy.*"

He paused for a moment to let his words sink in.

Then he cleared his throat, smiled one more time and said, "Without further adieu, it's my pleasure to present the *Blue Academy* Award for Best Director of a film that does not yet exist."

As the audience roared, the substitute teacher-turned-director-for-one-night walked down to the front of the theater where Mr. Brooks presented him the trophy -- a milkshake glass that had been painted gold by the kids.

As he looked out at the crowd giving him a standing ovation, Greg couldn't help but notice his mother, father and sister leading the applause.

His road had been so up-and-down over the years -- and he walked away from the kind of certain future that parents usually want for their child -- but his family knew this was his dream, and in the end, even if they didn't understand it, they just wanted to see him achieve it and be happy.

With tears in his eyes, Greg raised up the glass just like it was a real trophy and gave the acceptance speech whose first six words he practiced all his life.

"I'd like to thank the Academy...."

**

After the crowd went home, Greg headed over to The Tempo Cafe.

As he walked in, George, the manager, said, "How'd the movie go?"

Greg smiled and said, "It went well -- except that I was supposed to meet an old friend here a little while ago, and I lost all track of time."

With that said, he joined me in a booth by the window, set down his lunchbox briefcase and milkshake glass trophy, took off his shoes, said he was sorry for being late and then ordered the same thing he'd been having most all his life -- a grilled cheese sandwich and a vanilla shake.

As the clock struck twelve and 11-10-02 came to an end, Greg began to tell me the story of the first thirty years of his life.

The dreams he had. The goals he set. The books he read. The movies he loved. The teachers he admired. The rejections he faced. The mistakes he made. The obstacles he overcame. The kids he taught, the ones he learned from. The friends he found, the ones he lost. And above all else, a sense of what he thought others could learn from his unusual journey.

Because, as it turned out, *The First Thirty* didn't just refer to the first thirty years, or those first thirty goals, or even the first thirty Scholars his Foundation sent to college. It also referred to the first thirty lessons learned along the way -- including the one he learned the night he turned thirty when his story came to life right before everyone's eyes.

(30) Stick with a dream long enough, and it just might come true.

I had asked Greg just one question. Can you start at the beginning?

By the time he finished his answer, it was now well past five o'clock in the morning. The late-night crowd at The Tempo Cafe had long since left, and the early risers had not yet arrived. It was just about the only time of the day that the restaurant was not alive and hopping. In fact, there was only one other customer in the whole place -- a woman, probably in her mid-forties, sitting alone in the booth right next to us.

As I packed up my things, I apologized to Greg for asking a question whose answer required so much of his time.

He laughed and said, "Don't worry about it. I've watched the sun rise more than once over the last few years."

You might think he was just being polite, but he really didn't seem to mind. Because, at some point, shortly after he had finished the shake and the sandwich, he opened up his lunchbox, pulled out a pencil and paper and started drawing a picture of me while he told his story.

Every so often, he looked up at me -- studying my face intently, double-checking every crease, every shadow -- before turning his attention back to that paper and getting lost in the details of his work.

I am a self-conscious person and don't like being drawn, but in this instance, I didn't say a word -- knowing that Greg was a lot more likely to stick around and finish the story as long as there was something to distract him from thinking about how late it had gotten.

And so, I sat silent as the hours passed and he shared one chapter of his life after another. Until, finally, by the time it was five in the morning, he literally finished drawing two portraits at once.

The picture of his life that he painted for me, and the picture of me that he drew while doing it.

I thanked him again for the chance to tell his story and promised I'd do my best to tell it well.

"I know you will," he said. "I always have believed in you."

And with that, he put a tip on the table, tucked the paper and pencil back into his lunchbox, picked up his gold milkshake glass, rose from his seat, slipped on his shoes, wished me well and turned to leave.

As he did, the lady next to us suddenly waved and said, "You too."

"Excuse me?" Greg responded politely.

"Just now," she replied with a smile, "You said *take care of yourself.* You were looking out the window, but there's nobody else here, so I assumed you were talking to me, so I was just saying *you, too.*"

The woman was trying to be nice, but I sure didn't think Greg was going to take it that way. When we were little and people said they didn't see me, he launched into a tantrum loud enough to wake up the neighbors.

But I should point out, in fairness to Greg, that on this night, he didn't get upset at all. In fact, he didn't even correct the lady sitting next to us. He just smiled nicely and headed out the door.

Yesterday, if you would've told me that would be his reaction, I wouldn't have believed you. But now that I know where life has taken Greg in the twenty-five years since I last saw him, I'm not surprised at all.

Because if there's one thing he learned from his own story, it is that those who dare to dream -- those who recognize value where others see none, those who see the potential in something that does not yet exist -- will *always* encounter a person or two who don't see their vision.

And if *you* are a dreamer, I hope you remember that.

No matter how many people doubt what you can do, no matter how many doubt what you can see, don't give up on your vision.

Some people will look at the picture Greg drew on the night he turned thirty and say it's a portrait of his reflection in the window. But if you are a dreamer, you know better than that. You know he drew me.

Because anything your mind can think of can become a reality -- a film, a foundation, a friendship, *anything* -- if you're willing to spend the time it takes to make it come to life.

As Greg always says, *Imaginary* doesn't mean something doesn't exist. It means something doesn't exist *yet.* It *is* okay to dream.

And if *you* have a dream, and try to make it come to life just like Greg did, and run into a few more obstacles than you expect along the way just like he did, try to remember what his Grandma always said...

If life was nothing but straight lines, it wouldn't be worth living.

THE END

AFTER THOUGHTS

The next year, the Foundation had another Gala...back at Maggiano's.

At the event, the Foundation gave out its largest grant ever.
The grant was given to Blue Academy.
It was given to help their students learn how to make films.
Greg named the grant after the school's clerk.

At that same Gala, Jillip was honored as Volunteer of the Year.

The Milkshake Scholars attend schools all across the nation.
None of them have ever washed the glasses.

Greg eventually raised the price of his milkshakes to $10,000 each.
To justify the increased cost, he added one final ingredient which he
said captures the true essence of his foundation. A single nut on top.

When some people said Greg's shakes had gotten too expensive,
he created an alternative. For $1,000, you can meet him for a picture
with a used coffee cup. No actual coffee. Just you, him and the cup.

As of 11-10-02, Greg had never taken a salary from the Foundation.
He had still never set foot on an Ivy League campus, either.

To this day, the gold-painted milkshake glass sits by Greg's bed...along
with the menu from Harvard's and the book about Harriet Tubman.

The framed splinters of the rocking chair still hang above Greg's desk...
along with his portrait of Dr. King, the letter from Mr. Welton and the
honorary degree from Prairie State College.

When Greg's Grandma passed away, she left Greg a number of things.
One of them was a briefcase, but she didn't leave him the combination.
As of 11-10-02, he still had no idea what's inside.

On his 30th birthday, Greg announced his logo has a *fourth* meaning...
but as of this book's printing, he still has not revealed what it is.

Greg now spends much of the year speaking at schools, events and
companies around the country. He is also at work on his own first
book. He still draws portraits in his free time. And he still wears
mismatched socks every day.

-- To be continued --

CONTACT

Send us your thoughts about the story
Email **Feedback@TheFirstThirty.com**
**

For more on this book, go to **www.TheFirstThirty.com**
To make bulk orders, e-mail: **Books@IdeaListEnterprises.com**
**

To order copies of the expanded version of this book
geared toward adults, go to **www.TheSilhouetteMan.com**
**

For educators who want to base assignments on the story and/or parents
who want to discuss it with their kids, there is a Guide with hundreds of
questions, projects and ideas available at **www.APlaceToSit.com**
**

For more on Greg, go to **www.GregForbes.com**
**

To see a sample of Greg's artwork and learn more about having it exhibited
in your town or at your school, go to **www.MySleeplessNights.com**
**

To book Greg for a speech or event, e-mail **Events@GregForbes.com**
**

To be notified when additional books in this series are available,
including books geared toward youth, young adult and adult audiences,
e-mail **Books@IdeaListEnterprises.com**
**

www.WorldsGreatestName.com
Because the most important word in the world is your name
**

www.WorldsGreatestGrandma.com
Because everybody's got one.
**

To get a poster or shirt from the Film That Did Not Exist
go to **www.11-10-02.com**
**

For more information on The 11-10-02 Foundation,
go to **www.BrunchBunch.com**
**

To make a contribution ($5 and up) online to The 11-10-02 Foundation,
go to **www.BrunchBunch.com and click on Donate Now**
**

To get the current mailing address to make a contribution by mail, go to
www.BrunchBunch.com and click on Mailing Address

Pick up a pen - Fill out this page - Truly make this book your own

My first name is _____

Today's date is: _____ - _____ - _____

Pick One:

I'm under 30. My '11-10-02' (my 30th b-day) is _____ - _____ - _____

I'm over 30. My next '11-10-02' (my 60th or 90th) is: _____ - _____ - _____

Here's a list of three things I hope to accomplish before that date:

1. _____

2. _____

3. _____

When I look out my window, I see: _____

_____

I could improve the world outside my window if: _____

_____

Greg revealed that each part of his logo has a fourth meaning. What do you think they are? _____

_____

_____

Of the thirty lessons shared throughout this book, the one that I most want to (or need to) keep in mind every day is lesson # _____ because:

_____

_____

For more hundreds of other questions, projects and ideas, go to
www.APlaceToSit.com